Amie A Rich

A Journey to Rediscovering Yourself

Disclaimer

While every effort has been made to offer accurate advice, the content of this book is intended to educate and inspire you on your personal journey toward inner peace. I'm not a psychologist or medical doctor and do not offer any professional, health or medical advice. If you are suffering from a psychological or medical condition, please seek help from a qualified health professional.

Please note that the suggestions, exercises and practices outlined in this book are based on general practices and may not be suitable for every individual. Caution is to be taken, and the publisher and author are not responsible for actions taken. The intent of the author is only to offer information of a general nature to help you in your quest for emotional, physical, and spiritual well-being. In the event you use any of the information in the book for yourself, the author and the publisher assume no responsibility for your actions.

ISBN: 978-1-969463-60-0

Table of Contents

Introduction

Welcome, beautiful soul, to *The ABCs of Self-Love!*

If you're holding this book, chances are you're ready for a change—a shift towards embracing and celebrating the amazing person you are. Maybe you've been running on empty, always putting others first, or perhaps you've climbed the corporate ladder only to realize you've lost touch with the most important relationship in your life—the one with yourself.

I get it. I've been there, too.

My name is Amie Rich, and like many of you, I spent years striving for perfection, seeking validation from external sources, and feeling like I was never quite enough. With certifications in coaching, spiritual hypnotherapy, energy healing, life coaching, and Reiki, I bring a wealth of knowledge and experience to this book. I have juggled the demands of a high-powered career, motherhood, and countless other roles, all while burying my own needs and desires. It wasn't until I hit rock bottom of loneliness and depression that I realized something had to change. My journey to self-love wasn't easy, but it was the most rewarding path I've ever taken.

Why I Wrote This Book

The foundation of any successful personal growth journey starts with self-love. This isn't just a cliché. It's a profound truth that has transformed my life and the lives of many women I've had the honor to coach. How can we ever let love into our lives unless we truly love ourselves at the core? How can we give love to others authentically if we are not nurturing and honoring our own hearts?

Self-love is not about being self-centered or narcissistic; it's about recognizing your worth, embracing your flaws, and nurturing your soul. It's about treating yourself with the same kindness, respect, and compassion that you would offer to a close friend that you love. When we cultivate self-love, we create a solid foundation for all other relationships in our lives. We become better partners, parents, friends, and leaders.

This book is my heartfelt invitation for you to join me on this journey. Think of it as a playful and loving guide, where each letter of the alphabet represents a crucial aspect of self-love. From the gentle art of Acceptance to the peaceful embrace of Zen, we'll explore practical tips, fun exercises, and soul-nourishing affirmations that will help you reconnect with yourself in the most delightful ways.

Here's what you can expect as we embark on this adventure together:

Personal Stories and Insights

I'll share my own experiences and lessons learned along the way, making this journey feel like a heart-to-heart chat with a dear friend.

Practical Exercises

Each chapter is filled with actionable steps that you can easily incorporate into your daily life, from journaling prompts to creative activities.

Affirmations

You'll find powerful affirmations designed to uplift and inspire you on your path to self-love.

A Slice of Fun

Self-love doesn't have to be serious all the time! Expect a sprinkle of humor, playfulness, and joy throughout the book.

Whether you're new to the concept of self-love or looking to deepen your practice, this book is designed to be a safe and nurturing space for you to grow, heal, and thrive. Remember, this journey is uniquely yours—take what resonates, go at your own pace, and most importantly, be gentle with yourself.

So, grab a cozy blanket, your favorite beverage, and let's dive into this beautiful journey of self-discovery. Together, we'll uncover the radiant, empowered, and joyful person you are truly meant to be.

With love and light,
Amie Rich

How This Book is Structured and How to Use It

The ABCs of Self-Love is designed to be your personal guide to nurturing a deeper, more loving relationship with yourself. The most important takeaway from this book is to have fun. Each chapter corresponds to a letter of the alphabet, with each letter representing a key aspect of self-love. Here's a quick overview of how the book is structured:

A to Z Chapters: Each chapter dives into a specific theme, such as Acceptance, Boundaries, Compassion, and Zen. These themes are explored through personal stories, practical tips, affirmations, and exercises that you can easily incorporate into your daily life. Throughout the book, I share my own journey, and these stories are meant to inspire and remind you that you are not alone.

Each chapter includes actionable steps and journal prompts designed to help you apply the concepts of self-love in tangible ways. You'll also find powerful affirmations to support your practice and help you cultivate a loving mindset. And because this journey is meant to be fun, expect a touch of humor and joy throughout the book, making your self-love journey enjoyable and light-hearted.

How to Use This Book Effectively

This book is meant to be read at your own pace and be a companion on your journey. Feel free to read it cover to cover or jump to the chapters that resonate most with you at any given time.

The practical exercises are designed to help you integrate self-love into your daily life. Take your time with them and revisit them as needed. Use the journal prompts to deepen your self-awareness and track your progress. Reflection is a powerful tool for growth. Self-love is a practice that grows stronger with consistency. Incorporate the affirmations and exercises into your routine to create lasting change.

But remember... have fun! This journey is about celebrating and embracing yourself. Allow yourself to enjoy the process and find joy in your growth. This journey is uniquely yours—take what resonates, go at your own pace, and most importantly, be gentle with yourself.

Chapter One: A – Acceptance

Embrace Who You Are Without Judgment

Welcome to the first step on our journey: **ACCEPTANCE!**

Picture this... You are standing in front of a mirror and greeting your reflection with a big, warm smile. Acceptance is all about acknowledging and loving every part of yourself—your fabulous strengths, your quirky habits, and even those little flaws that make you uniquely you. It's saying, "Hey, this is me, and I am totally awesome just the way I am!"

Why Acceptance is Important

Acceptance is like the magic key to unlock your self-love adventure. It sets you free from the exhausting race to perfection and the endless game of comparing yourself to others. When you accept yourself, you silence that nagging inner critic and make room for a whole lot of self-kindness and compassion. And guess what? When you're at peace with yourself, you shine brighter in every part of your life and your relationships become richer and more authentic.

But let's get real for a second. Recognizing when acceptance isn't at the forefront of your thoughts can be a game-changer. Here are some common feelings that can help signal a lack of self-acceptance:

Constant Self-Criticism

You find yourself nitpicking every little detail about yourself, never feeling good enough.

Comparing Yourself to Others

You often measure your worth against others and feel you always come up short.

Fear of Judgment

You worry excessively about what others think of you, leading to people-pleasing behaviors.

Difficulty Embracing Mistakes

You beat yourself up over mistakes, viewing them as failures rather than learning opportunities.

Perfectionism

You set impossibly high standards for yourself and feel overwhelmed trying to meet them.

How to Embrace Who You Are Without Judgment

Acknowledge You

Take a moment each day to celebrate everything that makes you, you. The good, the messy, the extraordinary. Embrace it all!

Practice Self-Compassion

Imagine talking to yourself like you would to your best friend. Replace those harsh thoughts with words of kindness and encouragement.

Let Go of Comparisons

Remember, your journey is your own special adventure. Comparing yourself to others is like comparing apples to oranges—totally pointless!

Flaunt your quirks and celebrate what sets you apart. Your uniqueness is your superpower! Own it, because it's uniquely yours.

Reflective Journal Prompts

- What are three things I appreciate about myself today?
- When do I find myself being most critical of myself? How can I shift these thoughts to be more compassionate?
- What unique qualities do I bring to the world? How can I celebrate these more?
- How do I typically respond to my mistakes? How can I approach them with more acceptance and kindness?

> **Daily Affirmations for Acceptance**
>
> I am enough just as I am.
>
> I accept and love all parts of myself.
>
> I let go of self-judgment and embrace self-compassion.
>
> I honor my journey and my growth.
>
> I celebrate my uniqueness and my strengths.

- Reflect on a time when you felt fully accepted by someone else. How did that make you feel? How can you offer that same acceptance to yourself?

Embracing acceptance isn't about ignoring your flaws or never striving for improvement. It's about recognizing that you are a work in progress, and that's perfectly okay. So, next time you catch a glimpse of yourself in the mirror, give yourself a wink, smile and say, "I am enough, just as I am!"

As you embrace the power of Acceptance, remember that it's a journey, not a destination. Every day offers a new opportunity to practice self-compassion and celebrate your unique qualities. Now that you've started this journey by embracing who you are, it's time to protect and nurture this newfound self-love.

The next step on our journey is all about setting healthy Boundaries. Boundaries are essential for maintaining your well-being and ensuring that your relationships are supportive and balanced. So, let's dive into the art of saying "no" and creating space for what truly matters in your life.

Chapter Two: B – Boundaries

The Art of Saying "No" and Creating Space for What Truly Matters

Welcome to the world of **BOUNDARIES**!

Imagine your life as a gorgeous garden. Boundaries are the fences that protect your precious plants (your time, energy, and well-being) from being trampled by others. They help you keep out the weeds (stress, overwhelm, and negativity) and ensure that your garden flourishes with only the best care.

Why Boundaries are Important

Boundaries are essential for maintaining your mental, emotional, and physical health. They empower you to take charge of your life and prioritize what truly matters to you. Without boundaries, you might find yourself feeling drained, overcommitted, and resentful. But with clear, loving boundaries, you create a safe space where you can grow, thrive, and shine your brightest.

Setting boundaries can be challenging, especially if you're used to people-pleasing or putting others' needs before your own. But can I let you in on a secret? Boundaries aren't about shutting people out. They're about letting the right people and experiences in. When you set boundaries, you're teaching others how to treat you and showing yourself the respect you deserve.

How to Set and Maintain Healthy Boundaries

Know Your Limits

Take some time to reflect on what's important to you and what drains your energy. Recognize where you need to set boundaries to protect your well-being. Boundaries are all about what YOU need.

Communicate Clearly

Be honest and direct when expressing your boundaries. Use "I" statements to convey your needs without blaming or accusing others. Here is an example of an "I" statement for any single moms our there also climbing the corporate ladder.

"I value the quality time I spend with my children in the evenings, and I need to ensure I am available for them after work. I am committed to giving my best during my workday, so I would appreciate it if we could address any urgent matters within regular working hours. This way, I can maintain a healthy balance between my professional responsibilities and my family commitment's"

Stay Consistent

Consistency is key in maintaining boundaries. If you let them slide, it sends mixed messages to others and can lead to broken boundaries. Because boundaries are all about your needs, when you let others disrespect your wishes, they are disrespecting you.

Practice Self-Respect

Remember that setting boundaries is a form of self-respect. It's okay to say "no" to things that don't serve your highest good. It's very important to stand your ground when it comes to the boundaries that you set.

Personal Story

When I went through my divorce, I quickly realized the importance of setting boundaries to protect my emotional well-being and maintain a sense of stability for my children. One of my boundaries I had to establish was around communication with my ex-husband. To avoid unnecessary conflicts and maintain a peaceful environment for my kids, we would only discuss matters related to our children when our children weren't around. We agreed to keep our conversations focused on the kids and to communicate via call or text for less urgent matters, which helped reduce stress and miscommunication.

As a single mom, setting boundaries with my children became equally important. I wanted to ensure they felt loved and supported while also teaching them the value of respecting others' needs. For example, I established specific times for family activities and personal downtime. This not only gave my children a sense of routine and security but also allowed me to recharge and practice self-care. I also made it a point to involve my children in discussions about boundaries. We had open discussions to help them understand why certain limits were necessary and encouraging them to express their own needs and preferences.

Another significant boundary I set with myself was around money. I wanted to buy them whatever they wanted to keep them happy. Our finances were very tight, and we didn't have a TV for a long time. By having conversations with them about what our plans were, and why we were doing the things we did, helped hold me accountable to them. And it's ok to be vulnerable with your children. They are going to see right through your façade, anyway, so be open and honest with them.

Reflective Journal Prompts

- Where in my life do I feel overwhelmed or resentful? How can setting boundaries help?
- What are my non-negotiables when it comes to my time and energy?
- How do I feel when someone respects my boundaries? How do I feel when they don't?
- What is one boundary I need to set this week to protect my well-being?
- Reflect on a time when you successfully set a boundary. How did it improve your situation?

> **Daily Affirmations for Boundaries**
>
> I have the right to set healthy boundaries.
>
> My boundaries protect my well-being and my happiness.
>
> Saying "no" to others is saying "yes" to myself.
>
> I deserve relationships that respect my boundaries.
>
> I am confident in expressing my needs and limits.

As you embrace the power of Boundaries, remember that they are an essential part of your self-love toolkit. They help you protect your energy, honor your needs, and create a life that feels balanced and fulfilling. By setting and maintaining healthy boundaries, you're paving the way for deeper, more meaningful connections with yourself and others.

Now that we've mastered the art of saying "no" and creating space for what truly matters, let's move on to the next exciting step in our journey: Compassion. In the next chapter, we'll explore how to shower yourself with the kindness and understanding you so freely give to others.

Ready to dive into the world of Compassion? Let's go!

Chapter Three: C - Compassion

Shower Yourself with Kindness and Understanding

Welcome to the heartwarming world of **COMPASSION!**

Imagine wrapping yourself in a cozy, soft blanket of kindness. Imagine the softest blanket you can and then wrap yourself in the loving embrace of the warm blanket. Compassion is all about treating yourself with the same warmth, care, and understanding that you would offer a dear friend in their time of need. It's about being gentle with yourself, especially during times of struggle and self-doubt.

Why Compassion is Important

Compassion is a superpower that can transform your relationship with yourself. It allows you to embrace your imperfections and mistakes without harsh judgment. When you practice self-compassion, you create a safe space within your heart where you can heal, grow, and thrive. It's the antidote to self-criticism and the key to unlocking deeper self-love.

Life can be tough, and it's easy to fall into the trap of being your own worst critic. Recognizing the need for compassion is crucial, especially when you:

Beat Yourself Up for Mistakes

We all make mistakes, but constantly berating yourself only adds to your stress and lowers your self-esteem.

Feel Overwhelmed

Life's demands can be overwhelming, and being kind to yourself during these times can make all the difference.

Struggle with Self-Worth

If you often feel unworthy or not good enough, compassion can help you see your true value and worth.

How to Practice Self-Compassion

Speak Kindly to Yourself

Replace negative self-talk with words of kindness and encouragement. Imagine how you would comfort a friend in a similar situation and use those words for yourself. For example, if you're feeling down, say to yourself, "It's okay to feel this way. I'm doing my best, and that's enough."

Acknowledge Your Feelings

It's okay to feel sad, frustrated, or anxious. Accepting your emotions without judgment is a vital part of self-compassion. Try writing in a journal about how you're feeling, allowing yourself to express your emotions freely. The key is not judging your thoughts when you are feeling frustrated. Give yourself grace!

Give Yourself Permission to Rest

Listen to your body and mind. If you need a break, take it without feeling guilty. Rest is essential for your well-being. For instance, take a relaxing bath, enjoy a quiet cup of tea, or simply take a nap when you're feeling overwhelmed.

Celebrate Small Wins

Every step forward, no matter how small, is worth celebrating. Acknowledge your efforts and progress. For example, reward yourself with a small treat or take a moment to reflect on all your achievements at the end of your busy day.

Engage in Self-Care Activities

Dedicate time to activities that nourish your body and soul. This could include things such as practicing yoga, meditating, reading a good book, going for a walk in nature, or doing something creative like painting or crafting.

Practice Mindfulness

Spend a few minutes each day being present and mindful. This could be achieved through deep breathing exercises, mindful eating, or simply sitting quietly and observing your thoughts without judgment.

Create a Self-Compassion Ritual

Develop a daily or weekly ritual that focuses on self-compassion. This could be a gratitude journal, a nightly self-affirmation routine, or a special self-care day where you pamper yourself.

Reflective Journal Prompts

- How do I typically speak to myself when I make a mistake? How can I change this to be more compassionate?
- What are some ways I can show myself kindness today?
- Reflect on a time when you were compassionate towards a friend. How can you offer that same compassion to yourself?
- Write about a recent challenge and how practicing self-compassion helped (or could have helped) you through it.
- What does self-compassion mean to me, and how can I incorporate it into my daily life?

Daily Affirmations for Compassion

I am worthy of love and kindness.

I treat myself with the same compassion I offer to others.

I forgive myself for my mistakes and learn from them.

I honor my feelings and give myself the care I need.

I am patient and gentle with myself on this journey.

As you embrace the power of Compassion, remember that kindness starts within. By showering yourself with understanding and care, you build a strong foundation for self-love and resilience. Compassion allows you to navigate life's ups and downs with grace and strength, making your journey more fulfilling and joyful.

Now that we've wrapped ourselves in the cozy blanket of Compassion, it's time to dream big! In the next chapter, we'll dive into the magical world of Dreams, exploring how to pursue your passions and aspirations with courage and clarity.

Ready to chase those dreams?

Chapter Four: D - Dreams

Chase Your Dreams and Manifest Your Wildest, Imaginative Visions

Welcome to the dazzling world of **DREAMS**!

Imagine a sky full of glittering stars, each one representing a dream waiting to be realized. Dreams are the fuel that ignites our passions and propels us forward on our journey of self-love and personal growth. They give us a sense of purpose and direction, lighting up our lives with possibility and hope.

Why Dreams are Important

Dreams are vital for several reasons. They inspire us to reach beyond our current reality and envision a future filled with endless possibilities. Dreaming allows us to tap into our creativity and imagination, pushing the boundaries of what we believe is possible. When we dream big, we give ourselves permission to aspire to greatness and pursue our deepest desires.

Manifesting our dreams is equally important. It's about turning those vivid, imaginative visions into reality. Manifestation involves setting clear intentions, believing in our potential, and taking actionable steps towards our goals. By aligning our thoughts, emotions, and actions with our dreams, we create a powerful force that brings our aspirations to life.

How to Chase and Manifest Your Dreams

Visualize Your Dreams

Take time to vividly imagine your dreams. Create a mental picture of what achieving them looks and feels like. The key here is feeling as if it's already here right now! This can be as simple as daydreaming or as detailed as creating a vision board with images and words that represent your goals.

Set Clear Goals

Break down your dreams into achievable goals. Write them down and create a plan of action. For example, if your dream is to start your own business, outline the steps you need to take, such as researching your market, finding your niche, creating a business plan, and finding funding. For this exercise, draw a ladder and each step in your goal is a step up the ladder. As you outline the steps that will bring you closer, add each to the ladder with your goal at the top.

Believe in Yourself

Cultivate a positive mindset and believe in your ability to achieve your dreams. Affirmations and self-encouragement can help build your confidence. Remind yourself daily, "I am capable of achieving my dreams."

Take Aligned Action

Dreams without action remain just dreams. Take consistent, inspired, and actionable steps towards your goals. Even small steps can lead to significant progress over time. Celebrate each milestone you reach, no matter how small.

Stay Persistent

The path to achieving your dreams may be challenging, but persistence is key. Embrace setbacks as learning opportunities and keep moving forward. Remember, every great achievement starts with a dream and the determination to see it through.

Reflective Journal Prompts

- What are my wildest, most imaginative dreams? How do they make me feel?
- What small steps can I take today to move closer to my dreams?
- Reflect on a time when you achieved a goal. What actions and mindset helped you succeed?
- What obstacles have held me back from pursuing my dreams? How can I overcome them?
- How can I stay motivated and inspired to keep chasing my dreams, even when faced with challenges?

Daily Affirmations for Dreams

I am capable of achieving my dreams.

My dreams are within my reach.

I take action every day towards my goals.

I believe in my potential and my vision.

I am worthy of manifesting my wildest dreams.

As you embrace the magic of Dreams, remember that your aspirations reflect your limitless potential. By dreaming big and taking steps to manifest those dreams, you are honoring your true self and creating a life filled with purpose and joy. Let your dreams guide you, inspire you, and remind you of the incredible possibilities that lie ahead. In the next chapter, Empowerment, we'll explore how to take charge of your life and make empowered decisions that align with your true self.

Ready to feel empowered? Let's go and step into your power!

Chapter Five: E - Empowerment

Step into Your Power and Make Empowered Decisions

Welcome to the enchanting realm of **EMPOWERMENT!**

Imagine yourself standing tall on a mountaintop, feeling the exhilarating rush of confidence and strength coursing through you. Empowerment is all about taking charge of your life, making decisions that align with your true self, and embracing your inner strength. It's about realizing that you have the power to shape your own destiny and create a life that reflects your deepest values and desires.

Why Empowerment is Important

Empowerment is crucial because it enables you to live authentically and confidently. When you feel empowered, you trust your abilities and believe in your potential. Empowerment allows you to set and achieve your goals, overcome challenges, and navigate life's ups and downs with resilience and grace. It's the foundation of self-efficacy, where you recognize that you have control over your choices and actions, leading to a more fulfilling and purpose-driven life.

What It Means to Be Empowered

Being empowered means experiencing unshakeable confidence. It's waking up each day knowing that you are capable and deserving of achieving your dreams. It's the feeling of standing firm in your decisions, even when faced with doubts or external pressures. Empowerment is the inner assurance that you can handle whatever comes your way, because you trust in your strengths and abilities.

Personal Story

I want to share a personal story about a time when I embraced empowerment in a profound way. For years, I was in a marriage that was no longer healthy for me or my children. The thought of divorce was daunting, filled with fears of judgment, guilt, and the uncertainty of single parenthood. However, deep down, I knew that making a change was essential for our well-being.

Empowerment, for me, meant recognizing that despite the hurt and the potential criticism from others, I had to prioritize the health and happiness of my family. It was about standing up for myself and my children, making the tough decision to end the marriage, and embarking on a path to a better, more peaceful life. This decision was not easy, but it was necessary. It was the ultimate act of self-empowerment. Knowing what needed to be done and having the courage to do it, regardless of how others might perceive it.

How to Step into Your Power

Know Your Values

Take a moment to reflect on what truly matters to you. What are your non-negotiables? Understanding your core values helps guide your decisions and actions. For example, if family is a core value, make sure your choices reflect the importance of spending quality time with your loved ones.

Set Clear Intentions

Empowerment involves setting clear intentions and goals. Think about what you want to achieve and outline actionable steps to get there. For instance, if your goal is to advance in your career, break it down into smaller steps such as acquiring new skills, seeking mentorship, or taking on new projects.

Cultivate a Positive Mindset

Your mindset plays a significant role in how empowered you feel. Practice positive self-talk and affirmations to build your confidence. Replace limiting beliefs with empowering ones, such as "I am capable of achieving my dreams." Imagine how it feels to truly believe in yourself—lighter, stronger, and more focused.

Take Responsibility

Empowerment means taking responsibility for your life. Acknowledge that you have the power to make choices and influence outcomes. Embrace accountability and learn from your experiences, both successes and setbacks. Picture yourself as the captain of your ship, steering it confidently through calm waters and storms alike.

Surround Yourself with Support

Build a network of supportive people who uplift and inspire you. Seek out mentors, friends, and communities that encourage your growth and empower you to be your best self. Imagine the warmth and strength that comes from being surrounded by those who believe in you and are your biggest cheerleaders.

Reflective Journal Prompts

- What are my core values, and how do they influence my decisions?
- Reflect on a time when you felt truly empowered. What contributed to that feeling?
- What limiting beliefs are holding me back from feeling empowered? How can I change them?
- What are my short-term and long-term goals? What steps can I take today to move closer to them?
- How can I build a supportive network that empowers me to be my best self?

> **Daily Affirmations for Empowerment**
>
> I am in control of my life and my choices.
>
> I have the power to create the life I desire.
>
> I trust in my abilities and my strength.
>
> I make decisions that align with my true self.
>
> I am worthy of achieving my goals and dreams.

As you step into the courageous world of Empowerment, remember that you are the author of your own story. Embrace your inner strength, trust your abilities, and make decisions that reflect your true self. Empowerment is about recognizing your worth and taking bold steps towards the life you envision.

Now that you're standing tall in your power, it's time to explore "F" for Forgiveness. In the following chapter, we'll dive into the healing power of Forgiveness, learning how to let go of past hurts and embrace a future filled with peace and freedom, and discover the transformative power of Forgiveness!

Chapter Six: F – Forgiveness

The Healing Power of Letting Go

Welcome to the soothing world of **FORGIVENESS!**

Imagine the weight of the world lifting off your shoulders, replaced by a sense of lightness and peace. Forgiveness is a powerful tool for healing and self-love. It's about releasing the grip of past hurts, letting go of resentment, and freeing yourself from the emotional baggage that holds you back. Forgiveness is not about condoning the actions that hurt you; it's about reclaiming your power and choosing peace over pain.

Why Forgiveness is Important

Forgiveness is essential for your emotional and mental well-being. Holding onto anger and resentment can drain your energy, affect your health, and prevent you from moving forward. By forgiving, you release negative emotions and make room for love, joy, and inner peace. It allows you to break free from the past and embrace a brighter, more empowered future.

Personal Story: *Forgiving Myself*

Forgiveness isn't just about letting go of the wrongs done by others; it's also about forgiving ourselves. When I decided to get a divorce, I struggled with feelings of guilt and shame. I worried about how others would perceive me and whether I was making the right choice for my

children. But deep down, I knew that choosing myself and creating a healthier environment for my kids was the right decision.

Forgiving myself for this choice was a crucial step in my journey to self-love. I had to let go of the guilt and recognize that prioritizing my well-being and my children's happiness was not only necessary but also an act of self-respect and empowerment. This forgiveness allowed me to embrace my decision fully, heal the pain from the past, and move forward with confidence and love for myself.

How to Embrace Forgiveness

Acknowledge Your Feelings

Start by acknowledging the pain and hurt you feel. Where is the feeling in your body? Recognize the location and give yourself permission to feel these emotions without judgment. Work in mediation and visualize the location of the feeling in your body. See it! What color is it? Then visualize you massaging that area until the color lessens in saturation. And when you feel better and the color is almost gone, or completely gone, write in a journal and document what you felt.

On a scale, how strong was the pain before your meditation, and after the mediation where was the pain on the scale? Journaling can be a helpful way to process these feelings.

Understand the Impact

Reflect on how holding onto resentment or guilt affects your life. Consider the ways it drains your energy, impacts your relationships, and hinders your personal growth. You can also address the energy of resentment and guilt with visualization.

During meditation, envision a white ball of healing light in front of you. Add all the feelings that are holding you back to that ball. Then send it away up to Heaven to be alchemized into love and light. Watch as the healing ball ascends and watch it disappear. This is something you can do yourself, or if you need assistance with an energy healing session, send me a message. I'm happy to help.

Choose to Forgive

Make a conscious decision to forgive. Understand that forgiveness is for your benefit, not necessarily for the person who hurt you. It's about freeing yourself from the emotional burden. It frees you from the chains of old wounds, enabling you to live fully in the present and move forward without the burden of unresolved emotions. And remember forgiveness is a key component of spiritual growth. It aligns you with higher principles of compassion, mercy, and grace. This spiritual alignment can bring a deeper sense of purpose and connection to something greater than yourself.

Practice Self-Compassion

Be kind and gentle with yourself during this process. Remember that forgiving yourself is just as important as forgiving others. Acknowledge that you are human and deserving of compassion. Forgiving yourself is an act of self-love and empowerment. It acknowledges your humanity and imperfections, giving you the strength to accept yourself fully. This self-acceptance is crucial for building a strong foundation of self-worth and confidence.

Release and Let Go

Find ways to release the negative emotions associated with the hurt. This could be through meditation, visualization, or a symbolic act like writing a letter and then tearing it up or burning it.

Exercise to symbolically let it go

This exercise involves writing down your feelings of anger, hurt, or resentment on paper and then performing a ritual to symbolically release them. This process can help you visualize and internalize the act of forgiveness, creating a tangible sense of relief and closure.

Steps to Perform the Exercise:

Find a Quiet Space

Choose a quiet, comfortable place where you can be alone without distractions. This could be your favorite spot in your home, a peaceful outdoor location, or anywhere you feel safe and relaxed.

Gather Your Materials

You'll need paper, a pen, and a safe method to dispose of the paper (such as a fireplace, a fireproof container, or a bowl of water).

Reflect on Your Emotions

Take a few moments to reflect on the negative emotions you're holding onto. Consider who or what has hurt you and how these feelings are impacting your life. Allow yourself to fully experience these emotions without judgment.

Write Down Your Feelings

Begin writing down your thoughts and feelings on the paper. Be honest and specific. You might write about situations that caused you pain, people who hurt you, or mistakes you've made that you haven't forgiven yourself for. Pour all your emotions onto the paper.

Set Your Intentions

After writing, take a moment to set your intention for forgiveness. Acknowledge that you are choosing to release these negative emotions for your own peace and well-being. Affirm your decision to forgive and let go.

Perform the Ritual

Burning*: If you choose to burn the paper, do so safely. Light the paper with a candle or match and place it in a fireproof container or fireplace. Please be responsible with the burning paper. As you watch the paper burn, visualize the negative emotions dissolving into the flames and disappearing.

Water: If you prefer water, submerge the paper in a bowl of water. Watch as the ink smudges and the papers disintegrate, symbolizing the release of your emotions.

Tearing: If burning or water isn't an option, tear the paper into tiny pieces. As you do, imagine each piece representing a fragment of your pain being torn away and discarded.

Release and Reflect: Once you've completed the ritual, take a few deep breaths and visualize yourself feeling lighter and freer. Reflect on the sense of relief and closure you feel. Spend a few moments in silence, appreciating the act of letting go.

Affirm Your Forgiveness

Finish the exercise by repeating a forgiveness affirmation. For example: "I release these negative emotions and choose forgiveness. I am free from the past and open to peace and healing."

*Disclaimer: The author nor the publisher shall be held liable (including but not limited to liability by reason of negligence) from the fire risk in the ritual. Disclaimer includes any loss, damage, cost or expense whether direct, indirect, consequential or special,

Practical Ways to Embrace Forgiveness Daily

Daily Reflection

Set aside a few minutes each day to reflect on any negative feelings or resentments you may be holding. Write them down in a journal and consciously choose to release them.

Forgiveness Meditation

Practice a simple forgiveness meditation where you visualize yourself letting go of grudges and embracing peace. Imagine sending love and light to those who have hurt you, and to yourself.

Affirmations

Use forgiveness affirmations daily. Repeat them in the morning to set a positive tone for the day and before bed to release any lingering negative emotions.

Mindful Breathing

When feelings of anger or resentment arise, take a moment to practice mindful breathing. Inhale deeply, acknowledging the emotion, and exhale, imagining it leaving your body.

Gratitude Practice

Cultivate a gratitude practice by writing down three things you are grateful for each day. Focusing on positive aspects of your life can help shift your mindset and make forgiveness easier.

Acts of Kindness

Perform random acts of kindness, both towards others and yourself. This helps foster a forgiving and compassionate mindset.

Forgiveness Ritual

Create a weekly forgiveness ritual. This could be lighting a candle, saying a prayer, or performing a small ceremony where you symbolically release any grudges or negative feelings from the week.

Reflective Journal Prompts

- What past hurts or resentments am I holding onto? How do they affect my life?
- How can forgiving myself for past mistakes help me grow and heal?
- Reflect on a time when you forgave someone. How did it make you feel?
- What steps can I take to start the process of forgiveness today?
- How can practicing forgiveness improve my relationships and overall well-being?

Daily Affirmations for Forgiveness

I forgive myself for past mistakes and embrace my journey.

I release anger and resentment to make room for love and peace.

I am deserving of forgiveness and compassion.

I choose to let go of past hurts and move forward with an open heart.

I forgive others to free myself from the burden of resentment.

As you embrace the healing power of Forgiveness, remember that letting go of past hurts is a gift you give to yourself. It's an act of self-love that allows you to move forward with a lighter heart and a clearer mind. By forgiving yourself and others, you open the door to a future filled with peace, joy, and endless possibilities.

Now that we've unlocked the power of Forgiveness, let's explore Gratitude. In the following chapter, we'll dive into the transformative practice of cultivating a gratitude mindset and how it can enhance your life in beautiful ways.

Ready to embrace gratitude? Let's do this.

Chapter Seven: G – Gratitude

Embrace the Magic of Being Thankful

Welcome to the glittering world of **GRATITUDE!**

Who doesn't love glitter? Imagine every thank you as a sparkly gem, brightening your path and filling your heart with warmth and joy. Gratitude is all about recognizing and appreciating the wonderful things in your life, both big and small. It's about shifting your focus from what's lacking to what's abundant and letting that sense of thankfulness transform your outlook on life.

Why Gratitude is Important

Gratitude is a superpower that can dramatically improve your mental and emotional well-being. It helps you cultivate a positive mindset, reduces stress, and enhances your overall happiness. By regularly practicing gratitude, you train your brain to notice and appreciate the good things in your life, making you more resilient and joyful.

How to Cultivate Gratitude

Gratitude isn't just about being thankful for the obvious things such as family, friends, and a roof over your head—though those are important too! It's also about appreciating the often-overlooked miracles that happen every day. For example, think about the incredible intricacies of your body: your heart beating tirelessly, your lungs breathing without conscious effort, and your digestive system working to nourish you.

These miraculous processes happen without a second thought and deserve your gratitude just as much as anything else.

Gratitude Journaling Challenge Exercise

Let's dive into a fun and transformative exercise to cultivate gratitude. Grab your favorite journal or a notepad, and let's start a "Gratitude Journaling Challenge"!

Steps to Perform the Exercise:

Find a special journal

Choose a journal that makes you happy. It could be a beautiful notebook, a simple diary, or even a digital app. This will be your dedicated space for gratitude.

Set a daily time

Pick a time each day to sit down and write in your gratitude journal. Morning or bedtime works best, but anytime that fits your schedule is perfect.

Write down three things

Each day, write down at least 3-5 things you're grateful for. Challenge yourself to go beyond the usual suspects like family, friends, and home. Dive deeper and get creative!

Include the miraculous

Think about the amazing things your body does without you even asking. For example, you could write, "I am grateful for my lungs, which breathe for me without thinking," or "I am thankful for my digestive system that nourishes me every day."

Be specific and reflective

The more specific you are, the better. Instead of just writing "I'm grateful for my health," you might write, "I'm grateful for my strong legs that carry me through my day," or "I'm thankful for my heart that beats steadily and keeps me alive."

Reflect on your entries

Take a moment to reflect on what you've written. Feel the gratitude in your heart and let it lift your spirits. Imagine those sparkly gems of gratitude filling your heart with warmth and light.

Reflective Journal Prompts

- What are three unique things I am grateful for today?
- How does practicing gratitude change my perspective on challenging days?
- Reflect on a recent moment when you felt deep gratitude. What triggered that feeling?
- What miraculous aspects of my body am I thankful for today?
- How can I incorporate more moments of gratitude into my daily routine?

Daily Affirmations for Gratitude

I am grateful for the abundance in my life.

I appreciate the small miracles that happen every day.

My heart is full of gratitude and joy.

I am thankful for my body and all it does for me.

Gratitude fills my life with positivity and happiness.

As you immerse yourself in the enchanting practice of Gratitude, remember that thankfulness is a powerful tool for transforming your life. By focusing on the positive and appreciating the miracles around you, both big and small, you invite more joy, peace, and abundance into your world.

Gratitude turns the ordinary into the extraordinary and helps you see the magic in every moment.

Now that we've basked in the glow of Gratitude, it's time to move on to H for Healing. Let's explore the journey of healing past wounds and embracing a path of self-recovery and renewal.

Chapter Eight: H – Healing

Healing Past Wounds and Embracing a Journey of Self-Recovery

Welcome to the transformative world of **HEALING**!

Imagine yourself as a radiant, vibrant flower, blossoming and thriving after the rain. Healing is about nurturing your mind, body, and soul, allowing yourself to recover from past wounds and embrace a brighter, healthier future. It's a journey of self-discovery and renewal, where you shed old layers and reveal your true, beautiful self.

Why Healing is Important

Healing is crucial because it allows you to move past pain and trauma, transforming those experiences into sources of strength and wisdom. It helps you break free from patterns that no longer serve you and paves the way for growth and fulfillment. By healing, you reclaim your power and create space for joy, peace, and love in your life.

Healing Modalities and How They Can Assist You

There are various healing modalities that can support you on your journey. Each offers unique benefits and approaches to help you achieve a state of balance and well-being. Let's explore some of these powerful techniques:

Energy Healing

Energy healing involves balancing the body's energy systems to promote physical, emotional, and spiritual well-being. Techniques such as Reiki can help clear blockages, restore energy flow, and enhance your body's natural healing abilities.

How It Can Assist You: Energy healing can leave you feeling rejuvenated and balanced, helping you release stress and emotional blockages. It promotes overall harmony and well-being.

Spiritual Hypnotherapy

Spiritual hypnotherapy uses guided hypnosis to access the subconscious mind and address deep-seated issues. It can help you uncover and heal past traumas, release limiting beliefs, and connect with your Higher Self.

How It Can Assist You: Hypnotherapy can lead to profound transformations and greater self-awareness, helping you explore your subconscious and heal past wounds.

Life Coaching

Life coaching focuses on setting and achieving personal and professional goals. It involves identifying obstacles, developing strategies, and creating actionable plans to help you reach your full potential.

How It Can Assist You: Life coaching can help you clarify your goals, overcome challenges, and create a roadmap for success. It supports building confidence, enhancing skills, and achieving dreams.

Inner Child Healing

Inner child healing involves addressing and healing childhood wounds that affect your present life. It's about reconnecting with your inner child, offering them love and compassion, and integrating their needs into your adult life.

How It Can Assist You: Inner child healing can help you connect with and nurture your inner child, heal past traumas, and foster a loving relationship with yourself.

Mindfulness and Meditation

Mindfulness and meditation practices help you stay present, reduce stress, and cultivate a sense of inner peace. These techniques can enhance your mental clarity, emotional stability, and overall well-being.

How It Can Assist You: Mindfulness and meditation practices can be tailored to your needs, helping you incorporate these practices into your daily routine for lasting benefits.

Tapping (EFT - Emotional Freedom Techniques)

Tapping, or EFT (Emotional Freedom Techniques), involves tapping on specific points on the body while focusing on an issue or emotion you want to address. This technique combines elements of cognitive therapy and acupressure to reduce stress and emotional pain.

How It Can Assist You: Tapping can help you release negative emotions, reduce anxiety, and promote healing from past traumas. It's a simple, yet powerful tool that you can use anytime, anywhere to manage stress and enhance emotional well-being.

Reflective Journal Prompts

- What past wounds or traumas do I need to heal? How have they impacted my life?
- How can energy healing or spiritual hypnotherapy assist me in my healing journey?
- Reflect on a time when you felt deeply connected to your inner child. How can you nurture that connection?
- What mindfulness or meditation practices can I incorporate into my daily routine to support my healing?
- How can life coaching help me achieve my personal and professional goals?

> **Daily Affirmations for Healing**
>
> I am open to healing and transformation.
>
> My past does not define me; I am free to create my future.
>
> I am worthy of love, peace, and happiness.
>
> My body, mind, and spirit are healing every day.
>
> I embrace my journey of self-recovery and renewal.

As a certified coach, spiritual hypnotherapist, and energy healer with expertise in life coaching and Reiki, I am here to guide you on your healing journey. If you're unsure which modality is best for you, I can help you explore and discover the most effective approach tailored to your unique needs and goals. You can find more about my services and book a session with me by visiting amierich.com.

As you embark on the healing journey, remember that healing is a process. It's about taking small, compassionate steps towards wholeness and embracing the transformative power within you. By exploring and integrating various healing modalities, you create a holistic approach to your well-being, paving the way for a vibrant and fulfilling life.

It's time to move on to one of my favorite topics, Intuition. In the following chapter, we'll explore the incredible power of trusting and developing your inner wisdom.

Let's learn how to connect with your intuition.

Chapter Nine: I – Intuition

Connecting with and Trusting Your Inner Wisdom

Welcome to the enlightening world of **INTUITION**!

Imagine having an inner compass, always pointing you towards your true north, guiding you with subtle nudges and whispers. Intuition is that powerful inner wisdom that helps you make decisions aligned with your deepest desires and values. It's about trusting the gut feelings and insights that arise from within, leading you towards a more authentic and fulfilling life.

Why Intuition is Important

Intuition is a vital aspect of self-awareness and decision-making. It allows you to tap into your subconscious mind, accessing knowledge and insights that might not be immediately apparent. Trusting your intuition can help you navigate life's complexities with confidence and clarity, making choices that resonate with your true self.

How to Connect with Your Intuition

Create Quiet Time

Intuition often speaks in whispers, so creating quiet time is essential. Spend a few moments each day in silence, away from distractions. This could be through meditation, sitting in nature, or simply enjoying a quiet cup of tea.

Practice Mindfulness

Being present in the moment enhances your ability to notice intuitive nudges. Engage in mindfulness practices such as mindful breathing, mindful walking, or simply being fully present in your daily activities.

Listen to Your Body

Your body can be a powerful intuitive tool. Pay attention to physical sensations and emotions. Notice how your body reacts in different situations—tightness in the chest, butterflies in the stomach, or a sense of peace can all be signals from your intuition.

Journal Your Thoughts

Keep a journal to record your thoughts, feelings, and intuitive insights. Writing helps you process and clarify your inner experiences, making it easier to recognize patterns and intuitive guidance.

Ask for Guidance

When facing a decision, ask your intuition for guidance. You can do this through meditation, by asking a question and waiting for the first thought or feeling that arises, or even by writing down the question and seeing what insights come up as you reflect.

Understanding the Clairs

Intuition can also manifest through the "clairs," which are various ways that divine guidance speaks to us. Understanding these can help you recognize how your intuition communicates:

Clairvoyance (Clear Seeing)

This is the ability to receive intuitive information through visual images. You might see symbols, visions, or flashes of light that provide guidance.

Clairaudience (Clear Hearing)

This involves receiving intuitive messages through auditory means. You might hear words, sounds, or music that offer insights.

Clairsentience (Clear Feeling)

This is the ability to sense or feel intuitive information. You might experience physical sensations or strong emotions that guide you. This may be a gut feeling.

Claircognizance (Clear Knowing)

This is the ability to know something intuitively without knowing how you know it. You might have sudden insights or knowledge about a situation or decision.

Clairalience (Clear Smelling)

This involves receiving intuitive information through scents. You might smell fragrances or odors that hold significance. This may be a smell of someone's perfume.

Clairgustance (Clear Tasting)

This is the ability to taste something intuitively. You might experience tastes that provide clues or messages.

How to Trust Your Intuition

Start Small

Begin by trusting your intuition in small decisions, like what to eat for dinner or which route to take to work. As you build confidence in these smaller choices, you'll find it easier to trust your intuition in bigger decisions.

Reflect on Past Experiences

Think about times when you followed your intuition, and the outcomes were positive. Reflecting on these experiences reinforces your belief in your inner wisdom.

Let Go of Doubt

It's natural to question your intuition, especially if you're used to relying on logic and external advice. Practice letting go of doubt by affirming that your intuition is a reliable guide.

Validate Your Feelings

When your intuition speaks, validate your feelings rather than dismissing them. Trust that your inner wisdom is looking out for your best interests.

Seek Alignment

Make decisions that align with your core values and desires. When your choices resonate with your true self, you reinforce the trust in your intuition.

Reflective Journal Prompts

- When have I followed my intuition, and what was the outcome?
- How do I feel when I trust my intuition versus when I ignore it?
- What small decisions can I start trusting my intuition with today?
- Reflect on a time when ignoring your intuition led to a less favorable outcome. What did you learn from that experience?
- How can I create more quiet time in my life to connect with my intuition?

Daily Affirmations for Intuition

I trust my inner wisdom and intuition.

My intuition guides me to make the best decisions.

I am connected to my inner voice and listen to its guidance.

My intuition is a powerful tool that supports my well-being.

I trust the signals and messages from my intuition.

As you deepen your connection with your Intuition, remember that your inner wisdom is always available to guide you. By creating space for quiet reflection, practicing mindfulness, and validating your intuitive feelings, you build a strong relationship with your inner compass. Trusting your intuition leads to more authentic and fulfilling decisions, allowing you to navigate life with confidence and clarity.

Chapter Ten: J- Joy

Finding Joy in Everyday Moments

Welcome to the vibrant world of **JOY**!

Imagine your life as a canvas, splashed with bright, cheerful colors that lift your spirits and warm your heart. Joy is all about finding happiness in the little things and cultivating a sense of delight in your daily life. It's about celebrating the moments that make you smile and embracing the experiences that fill your heart with laughter and light.

Why Joy is Important

Joy is a powerful emotion that can transform your life. It boosts your mood, strengthens your resilience, and enhances your overall well-being. By seeking out and savoring moments of joy, you create a positive mindset that attracts more happiness and fulfillment. Joy is the fuel that keeps your spirit alive, making life's journey more enjoyable and meaningful.

How to Cultivate Joy

Celebrate Small Wins

Take time to acknowledge and celebrate your achievements, no matter how small. Each step forward is a victory worth savoring.

Engage in Playful Activities

Find activities that bring out your inner child and make you laugh. Whether it's playing a game, dancing around your living room, or doing something creative, release the confines of adulthood and let yourself have fun.

Practice Gratitude

Gratitude and joy go hand in hand. Keep a gratitude journal and write down the things that bring you joy each day. Reflecting on these moments amplifies your happiness.

Spend Time with Loved Ones

Surround yourself with people who uplift and inspire you. Share joyful experiences and create happy memories together.

Be Present

Joy often resides in the present moment. Practice mindfulness and savor the here and now. Notice the beauty around you, the warmth of the sun, the sound of laughter—these little moments add up to a joyful life.

Personal Story

One of my favorite joyful memories involves being in Missouri during a quick passing thunderstorm. Being from California, I can appreciate a good rain and to be honest, I miss it. When the rainstorm started, I walked outside

and sat on the porch. I marveled at the wind and the force of the torrential downpour. The spontaneous decision to sit outside was one of joy and wonderment. It was as if my inner child wanted to play in the rain, and my adult-self said yes. My dad eventually came to find me, wondering why I was outside in the rain. He found me, smiled and went back inside. Though he didn't want to join me in the wet weather, he understood my deep desire to be free.

Reflective Journal Prompts

- What activities bring me the most joy, and how can I incorporate them into my daily routine?
- Reflect on a recent joyful moment. What made it special, and how did it make you feel?
- How can I create more opportunities for laughter and fun in my life?
- Who are the people that bring joy into my life, and how can I spend more time with them?
- What small wins can I celebrate today, and how can I acknowledge them?

> **Daily Affirmations for Joy**
>
> I find joy in the little moments of life.
>
> My heart is open to happiness and laughter.
>
> I create and celebrate joyful experiences every day.
>
> Joy flows through me and brightens my world.
>
> I embrace fun, playfulness, and delight in my life.

As you immerse yourself in the vibrant world of Joy, remember that happiness is a choice you can make every day. Let yourself be spontaneous. By celebrating small wins, engaging in playful activities, and cherishing the present moment, you cultivate a life filled with joy and positivity. Embrace the fun, laughter, and delight that surround you, and let joy be the guiding light on your journey.

Now that we've basked in the glow of Joy, and oh it feels good, it's time to move on to Kindness. In the following chapter, we'll explore the power of practicing kindness towards yourself and others, and how it can transform your life. Ready to spread some kindness?

Chapter Eleven: K – Kindness

Practicing the Power of Kindness Towards Yourself and Others

Welcome to the heartwarming world of **KINDNESS**!

Imagine kindness as a gentle breeze that touches everything it passes, leaving behind warmth and comfort. Kindness is all about showing compassion, understanding, and generosity towards yourself and others. It's the simple acts of love and care that can make a profound difference in someone's life, including your own.

Why Kindness is Important

Kindness is a powerful force that can transform your relationships, your community, and your inner world. It fosters connection, builds trust, and spreads positivity. When you practice kindness, you not only uplift others but also nourish your own soul. Acts of kindness release feel-good hormones, reduce stress, and enhance your overall well-being.

The Concept of Filling People's Buckets

Think of every person, including yourself, as carrying an invisible bucket. When you do something kind for someone, you fill their bucket, and in turn, it fills yours. This simple yet powerful concept illustrates the ripple effect of kindness. By filling others' buckets with acts of random kindness, you contribute to a cycle of positivity and joy. Conversely, when our own buckets are empty, it becomes challenging to show kindness. Therefore, it's essential to practice self-kindness to keep your own bucket full.

How to Practice Kindness

Be Kind to Yourself

Self-kindness is the foundation of all kindness. Treat yourself with the same compassion and understanding that you would offer a friend. This includes forgiving yourself for mistakes, speaking kindly to yourself, and taking time for self-care.

Perform Random Acts of Kindness

Simple gestures like holding the door open for someone, paying for a stranger's coffee, or offering a genuine compliment can brighten someone's day and create a ripple effect of positivity.

Listen with Empathy

Sometimes, the greatest act of kindness is to simply listen. Offer your full attention to others, validating their feelings and showing that you care.

Offer Your Help

Whether it's helping a neighbor with groceries, volunteering your time, or supporting a friend in need, offering your assistance is a meaningful way to practice kindness.

Spread Positivity

Share kind words, uplifting messages, and positive vibes. A heartfelt note, a cheerful text, or a smile can go a long way in spreading joy and kindness.

Reflective Journal Prompts

- How can I be kinder to myself in my daily life?
- Reflect on a recent act of kindness you experienced. How did it make you feel?
- What small acts of kindness can I incorporate into my routine?
- Who in my life could use a little extra kindness, and how can I offer it?
- How does practicing kindness towards others affect my own well-being?

Daily Affirmations for Kindness

I am kind and compassionate towards myself and others.

My actions and words spread kindness and positivity.

I embrace opportunities to show kindness every day.

Kindness flows naturally from my heart.

I make the world a better place through my acts of kindness.

Filling Buckets: The Joy of Kindness

As previously mentioned, when we perform acts of kindness, we fill others' buckets, and our own bucket gets filled in return. This mutual exchange of kindness creates a sense of fulfillment and joy. Imagine starting your day by filling someone's bucket with a kind word, a gesture or a simple smile. Not only do you brighten their day, but you also uplift your own spirit. Remember, you can't pour from an empty bucket, so make sure to keep your own bucket filled with self-kindness and self-care.

As you embrace the power of Kindness, remember that every act, no matter how small, contributes to a more compassionate and loving world. By showing kindness to yourself and others, you create a ripple effect of positivity and connection. Let kindness be the guiding force in your interactions and watch how it transforms your life and the lives of those around you.

Who's ready for some Love? In the next chapter, join me in a beautiful journey of embracing and embodying unconditional self-love. Ready to open your heart to love?

Chapter Twelve: L – Love

Understanding and Embodying Unconditional Self-Love

Welcome to the heart of your journey: **LOVE**!

Imagine your heart as a radiant sun, shining warmth and light not only onto others but also onto yourself. Love is the foundation of a fulfilling and joyful life. It's about embracing yourself wholly and unconditionally, recognizing your worth, and treating yourself with the same care and compassion that you offer to those you love.

Why Self-Love is Important

Self-love is the cornerstone of all personal growth and happiness. It empowers you to set healthy boundaries, make choices that align with your true self, and cultivate meaningful relationships. When you love yourself, you acknowledge your value and deserve happiness, respect, and kindness. Self-love is not about being self-centered; it's about creating a healthy relationship with yourself, which in turn enhances your ability to love and care for others.

How to Cultivate Self-Love

Practice Self-Compassion

Be gentle with yourself, especially during times of struggle. Acknowledge your imperfections and mistakes without judgment. Treat yourself with the same kindness you would offer a friend.

Set Healthy Boundaries

Self-love means respecting your needs and limits. Learn to say no to things that drain your energy or compromise your well-being. Boundaries protect your time, energy, and emotional health.

Nourish Your Body and Mind

Take care of your physical, mental, and emotional health. Eat nutritious foods, exercise regularly, get enough sleep, and engage in activities that bring you joy and relaxation.

Celebrate Your Accomplishments

Take time to acknowledge and celebrate your achievements, no matter how small. Recognize your progress and give yourself credit for your efforts.

Surround Yourself with Positive Influences

Spend time with people who uplift and support you. Let go of toxic relationships that undermine your self-worth and well-being.

Reflective Journal Prompts

- What do I love most about myself, and why?
- How can I practice self-compassion during difficult times?
- Reflect on a time when you felt truly loved and valued. How can you recreate that feeling for yourself?
- What boundaries do I need to set to protect my well-being?
- How can I nourish my body, mind, and spirit today?

Daily Affirmations for Self-Love

I am worthy of love and respect.

I embrace my imperfections and celebrate my uniqueness.

I treat myself with kindness and compassion.

I honor my needs and set healthy boundaries.

I love and accept myself unconditionally.

Embodying Unconditional Self-Love

Embodying unconditional self-love means accepting and loving yourself as you are, without conditions or exceptions. It's about embracing your strengths and acknowledging your flaws, understanding that both are part of what makes you uniquely you. When you practice self-love, you create a strong foundation for a happy and fulfilling life.

Reflecting on my own journey, I remember the pivotal moment when I realized the importance of self-love. After years of seeking validation from external sources, I finally understood that true love and acceptance must come from within. This realization transformed my life, enabling me to set healthy boundaries, pursue my passions, and build deeper, more meaningful relationships. Embracing self-love has been the most empowering and liberating experience of my life.

As you embrace and embody unconditional Self-Love, remember that you are deserving of all the love, kindness, and respect you offer to others. By cultivating a loving relationship with yourself, you create a solid foundation for a joyful and fulfilling life. Let love be the guiding light in your journey, illuminating your path with warmth and compassion.

What does it mean to be mindful? In the next chapter, we chat all things Mindfulness. We'll explore the practice of being present and fully engaged in the moment, enhancing your connection with yourself and the world around you.

Chapter Thirteen: M – Mindfulness

Embrace the Present Moment and Connect with Your Inner Self

Welcome to the serene world of **MINDFULNESS**!

Imagine your mind as a calm, clear lake, reflecting the beauty of the present moment. Mindfulness is all about being fully present and engaged in your life, cultivating awareness and acceptance of each moment without judgment. It's a practice that enhances your connection with yourself and the world around you, bringing peace and clarity to your mind.

Why Mindfulness is Important

Mindfulness is a powerful tool for reducing stress, enhancing emotional regulation, and improving overall well-being. By practicing mindfulness, you learn to quiet the constant chatter of your mind, focusing on the here and now. This presence allows you to respond to life's challenges with greater clarity and calmness. Mindfulness also deepens your self-awareness, helping you to better understand your thoughts, feelings, and behaviors.

How to Cultivate Mindfulness

Start with Breath Awareness

Begin by focusing on your breath. Take slow, deep breaths, and pay attention to the sensation of the air entering and leaving your body. This simple practice can anchor you in the present moment.

Engage Your Senses

Use your senses to ground yourself in the present. Notice the sights, sounds, smells, tastes, and textures around you. For example, savor the flavor of your morning coffee or feel the warmth of the sun on your skin.

Practice Mindful Eating

Eat your meals with full attention. Notice the colors, smells, and flavors of your food. Chew slowly and mindfully, appreciating each bite. This practice can enhance your enjoyment of food and improve digestion.

Incorporate Mindfulness into Daily Activities

Bring mindfulness to your everyday tasks, such as washing dishes, walking, or brushing your teeth. Focus fully on the activity, noticing each movement and sensation.

Meditate Regularly

Set aside time each day for meditation. Even a few minutes of sitting quietly, focusing on your breath or a mantra, can make a significant difference in your mindfulness practice.

Reflective Journal Prompts

- How do I feel when I am fully present in the moment?
- What activities help me cultivate mindfulness in my daily life?
- Reflect on a recent experience where you practiced mindfulness. How did it impact your mood and perspective?
- What thoughts or distractions often pull me away from the present moment? How can I gently bring myself back to mindfulness?
- How can I incorporate more mindfulness practices into my daily routine?

Daily Affirmations for Mindfulness

I am present in this moment.

I embrace the peace and clarity of mindfulness.

I am aware of my thoughts and feelings without judgment.

I find joy in the simple moments of life.

I am connected to the here and now.

The Practice of Mindfulness

Mindfulness is not about clearing your mind of thoughts but about noticing them without getting caught up in them. It's about observing your thoughts and feelings as they arise, without labeling them as good or bad. This non-judgmental awareness helps you stay grounded and centered, allowing you to respond to life with greater calm and intention.

As you embrace the practice of Mindfulness, remember that it is a journey of ongoing discovery and growth. By cultivating awareness and presence, you create a deeper connection with yourself and the world around you. Let mindfulness guide you towards a life filled with peace, clarity, and joy.

Are you ready to discover the importance of nurturing yourself and others, and how this practice can enhance your well-being and relationships? Ready to nurture and be nurtured?

Chapter Fourteen: N – Nurture

Nurturing Your Body, Mind, and Soul

Welcome to the comforting world of **NURTURE!**

Imagine yourself as a gardener, tending to a beautiful garden with love and care. Nurturing is all about providing the support, attention, and kindness needed for growth and flourishing. To nurture someone truly means to provide care, support, and encouragement in a way that helps them grow, thrive, and feel valued. It involves attending to their physical, emotional, and psychological needs with compassion and understanding. Nurturing someone goes beyond basic care; it's about creating an environment where they feel safe, loved, and empowered to reach their full potential.

Why Nurturing is Important

Nurturing is essential for emotional and physical well-being. It helps build resilience, fosters healthy relationships, and promotes personal growth. By nurturing yourself, you replenish your energy and cultivate self-love. By nurturing others, you build strong, supportive connections that enhance mutual well-being. Nurturing is the foundation of a compassionate and fulfilling life.

How to Nurture Yourself

Prioritize Self-Care

Make self-care a non-negotiable part of your routine. This includes regular exercise, healthy eating, sufficient sleep, and activities that bring you joy and relaxation.

Practice Self-Compassion

Be gentle with yourself. Acknowledge your feelings and experiences without judgment. Treat yourself with the same kindness and understanding you would offer a dear friend.

Create a Peaceful Environment

Surround yourself with things that bring you peace and comfort. This could be a cozy home, a serene workspace, or a quiet corner where you can relax and recharge.

Engage in Activities You Love

Spend time doing things that make you happy and fulfilled. Whether it's reading, painting, hiking, or cooking, make time for activities that nurture your soul.

Set Healthy Boundaries

Protect your time and energy by setting boundaries that prioritize your well-being. Learn to say no to things that drain you and yes to things that uplift you.

How to Nurture Others

- Express your love and concern through actions and words. Listen actively and giving your full attention, showing empathy, and validating their feelings without judgment.
- Being a source of positive reinforcement. Encourage others to pursue their dreams and celebrate their achievements, big or small.
- Being a comforting presence during difficult times. Offer a listening ear, a shoulder to cry on, and words of reassurance.

- Spending quality time with loved ones. Create memories together through shared activities, conversations, and celebrations.
- Practicing small acts of kindness can have a big impact. Whether it's a smile, a kind word, or a thoughtful gesture, spread kindness to nurture those around you.

Reflective Journal Prompts

- How can I incorporate more self-care into my daily routine?
- Reflect on a time when you felt nurtured by someone else. What did they do, and how did it make you feel?
- What activities bring me joy and fulfillment? How can I make more time for them?
- Who in my life could use a little extra nurturing, and how can I offer it?
- How do I feel when I practice self-compassion and self-care?

Daily Affirmations for Nurturing

I nurture myself with love and compassion.

I create a peaceful and supportive environment for myself and others.

My actions and words nourish those around me.

I prioritize self-care and well-being.

I am a source of encouragement and support for others.

The Practice of Nurturing

Nurturing yourself and others is a continuous practice of care and compassion. It's about recognizing the needs of your mind, body, and spirit, and taking steps to meet those needs. By nurturing yourself, you build a strong foundation for personal growth and well-being. By nurturing others, you contribute to a supportive and loving community.

Reflecting on my journey, I've learned that nurturing is an act of love that starts within. When I prioritize self-care and compassion, I am better equipped to support and nurture those around me. This practice has transformed my relationships and enriched my life, creating a ripple effect of positivity and care.

As you embrace the practice of Nurturing, remember that care and compassion are powerful tools for personal and collective well-being. By nurturing yourself and others, you create a life filled with love, support, and joy. Let nurturing be the guiding force that helps you and those around you flourish.

In the following chapter, we'll discover the power of maintaining a positive outlook and how it can transform your life. Ready to embrace "O" for optimism?

Chapter Fifteen: O – Optimism

Embrace the Power of a Positive Outlook

Welcome to the uplifting world of **OPTIMISM**!

Imagine your mind as a clear, bright sky, filled with sunshine and endless possibilities. Optimism is about maintaining a positive outlook on life, focusing on the good, and believing in the best possible outcomes. It's a mindset that empowers you to navigate challenges with resilience and hope, creating a life filled with joy and fulfillment.

Why Optimism is Important

Optimism is a pivotal part of raising your vibration and enhancing your overall well-being. When you adopt an optimistic mindset, you align yourself with higher vibrational energies, attracting positivity and abundance into your life. This positive energy not only boosts your mood but also strengthens your immune system, reduces stress, and improves your mental health. Optimistic people are more resilient in the face of adversity, as they believe in their ability to overcome obstacles and achieve their goals. By cultivating optimism, you create a positive environment for growth, happiness, and success.

How to Cultivate Optimism

Practice Gratitude

Regularly acknowledge and appreciate the good things in your life. Keep a gratitude journal where you write down things you're thankful for each day. Focusing on gratitude shifts your mindset towards positivity and raises your vibration.

Reframe Negative Thoughts

When negative thoughts arise, consciously reframe them into positive or neutral ones. For example, instead of thinking, "I can't do this," tell yourself, "This is challenging, but I can find a way to succeed." This shift in perspective elevates your energy and keeps you aligned with positive outcomes.

Surround Yourself with Positivity

Spend time with positive, supportive people who uplift and inspire you. Avoid negative influences that drain your energy and dampen your spirit. Your environment greatly impacts your vibrational energy.

Visualize Success

Imagine yourself achieving your goals and experiencing positive outcomes. Visualization strengthens your belief in your abilities and motivates you to act. This powerful practice helps manifest your desires into reality by aligning your thoughts with your goals.

Celebrate Small Wins

Acknowledge and celebrate your achievements, no matter how small. Each step forward is a victory that reinforces your optimistic mindset and keeps your vibration high.

Reflective Journal Prompts

- What are three things I am grateful for today, and how do they make me feel?
- Reflect on a recent challenge. How did maintaining a positive outlook help me navigate it?
- What negative thought patterns do I need to reframe, and how can I turn them into positive ones?
- Who in my life brings positivity and joy, and how can I spend more time with them?
- How can I celebrate my small wins and acknowledge my progress?

Daily Affirmations for Optimism

I am optimistic about the future and trust in my path.

Positive energy flows through me and around me.

I see the good in every situation and learn from challenges.

My optimistic outlook attracts success and happiness.

I can achieve great things.

The Practice of Optimism

Optimism is not about ignoring life's difficulties; it's about approaching them with a positive and hopeful mindset. It's about finding the silver lining in every cloud and believing in your ability to create a better future. By practicing optimism, you build resilience and a strong foundation for personal growth and happiness.

As you embrace the power of Optimism, remember that a positive outlook can transform your life. By focusing on the good, reframing negative thoughts, and celebrating your achievements, you create a mindset that attracts joy, success, and fulfillment. Let optimism guide you through life's challenges and open the door to endless possibilities.

Now that we've explored the uplifting power of Optimism and raising your vibration, let's talk about finding inner Peace. We'll discover how to cultivate inner peace and maintain a sense of calm amidst life's chaos. See you there.

Chapter Sixteen: P – Peace

Cultivate Inner Peace and Maintain Calm Amidst Life's Chaos

Imagine a tranquil pond, its surface smooth and undisturbed, reflecting the calm sky above. **PEACE** is about finding and maintaining a sense of calm and tranquility within yourself, regardless of external circumstances. It's about creating a sanctuary in your mind and heart where you can retreat and recharge.

Why Peace is Important

Inner peace is essential for mental and emotional well-being. It helps reduce stress, anxiety, and overwhelm, allowing you to navigate life's challenges with clarity and grace. When you cultivate inner peace, you create a stable foundation for joy, resilience, and personal growth. Peaceful moments recharge your spirit, enhance your focus, and improve your relationships.

How to Cultivate Inner Peace

Practice Mindfulness and Meditation

Set aside time each day for mindfulness or meditation. Focus on your breath, let go of distractions, and allow yourself to be fully present. This practice calms your mind and centers your thoughts.

Simplify Your Life

Reduce clutter and simplify your surroundings. Create a peaceful environment at home and work. Simplifying your commitments and focusing on what truly matters helps to reduce stress and promote peace.

Set Healthy Boundaries

Protect your peace by setting boundaries that honor your well-being. Learn to say no to things that drain your energy and yes to activities and relationships that nurture your soul.

Engage in Relaxation Activities

Find activities that help you relax and unwind. This could be taking a walk in nature, practicing yoga, reading a good book, or listening to calming music. Make relaxation a regular part of your routine.

Cultivate Gratitude

Focus on the positive aspects of your life and express gratitude for them. Keeping a gratitude journal helps shift your perspective towards the positive and fosters a sense of peace.

Reflective Journal Prompts

- What activities or practices help me feel at peace?
- Reflect on a recent moment of peace. What made it special, and how did it make you feel?
- How can I simplify my life to create more space for peace?
- What boundaries do I need to set to protect my peace?
- How can I incorporate more moments of gratitude into my daily routine?

Daily Affirmations for Peace

I am calm and centered.

Peace flows through me with every breath.

I create a tranquil space within my mind and heart.

I am at peace with myself and the world around me.

I protect my peace by honoring my needs and boundaries.

The Practice of Peace

Peace is not just the absence of conflict but the presence of tranquility and harmony within yourself. It's about finding stillness in the midst of chaos and maintaining a calm heart no matter what life throws your way. By practicing peace, you cultivate a sense of stability and resilience that helps you navigate life's ups and downs with grace.

As you cultivate inner Peace, remember that tranquility begins within. By embracing mindfulness, simplifying your life, and setting healthy boundaries, you create a serene space in your mind and heart. Let peace be your guide, helping you navigate life's challenges with calm and grace, and enriching your journey with moments of deep tranquility.

The importance of prioritizing Quality in all aspects of your life, from relationships to personal growth, is the key to serenity and deep healing. Ready to enhance your life with quality?

Chapter Seventeen: Q – Quality

Prioritize Quality in All Aspects of Your Life

Welcome to the enriching world of **QUALITY**!

Imagine your life as a finely crafted tapestry, woven with care and intention. Quality is about choosing excellence in everything you do, from your relationships to your personal growth. It's about valuing depth over breadth, and substance over superficiality, creating a life filled with meaning and fulfillment.

Why Quality is Important

Prioritizing quality enhances your overall well-being and satisfaction. It ensures that you invest your time, energy, and resources in things that truly matter, bringing lasting joy and value to your life. Quality relationships, experiences, and self-care practices contribute to your happiness, resilience, and personal growth.

Quality Over Perfection

It's important to remember that prioritizing quality does not mean striving for perfection. Quality is about making intentional choices that add value and meaning to your life, not about everything being flawless. Embracing quality means appreciating the beauty in imperfection and recognizing that growth and fulfillment often come from experiences that are real and authentic, not perfect.

How to Cultivate Quality

Invest in Meaningful Relationships

Choose to surround yourself with people who uplift, support, and inspire you. Nurture relationships that bring mutual growth and joy. Let go of toxic connections that drain your energy.

Pursue Excellence in Your Work

Strive to do your best in your professional endeavors. Focus on quality over quantity and take pride in your work. Continuous learning and improvement contribute to a fulfilling career.

Practice Mindful Consumption

Be intentional about what you bring into your life, from the food you eat to the media you consume. Choose high-quality, nourishing options that support your well-being.

Engage in Enriching Activities

Spend your time on activities that bring you joy, growth, and fulfillment. Whether it's a hobby, a new skill, or a meaningful project, prioritize activities that enhance your life.

Prioritize Self-Care

Make self-care a quality practice. Choose activities that genuinely replenish your energy and well-being and avoid superficial quick fixes that don't contribute to long-term health.

Personal Story: *Quality over Quantity*

After my divorce, the kids and I had a 2-bedroom apartment. It wasn't ideal for them to share a bedroom, but we were also missing many other luxuries that they were used to. We did not have a television, as money was tight. We did not eat out and our play time was spent being creative and active. These times were stressful for me as I wanted to provide everything I could for my children. Shifting to the co-parenting dynamic was already a major change for them, and I did not want them to feel that they were less-than in any way. So, I made up for that lack of material items with my time. I made sure that we played games, swam in the community pool and had picnics in the park. We covered miles of bike paths as we rode our bikes or scooters and spent quality time together. Now that they are older, they remember this time in their lives with fond memories. What I assumed would be a time of sadness for them, ended up being such a great bonding time for them. It was choosing quality over quantity that won out for all of us.

Reflective Journal Prompts

- What areas of my life would benefit from a focus on quality over quantity?
- Reflect on a high-quality relationship or experience. What made it special, and how did it impact your life?
- How can I bring more quality into my daily routines and habits?
- What changes can I make to ensure I am consuming high-quality, nourishing content?
- How can I prioritize self-care in a way that truly enhances my well-being?

> **Daily Affirmations for Quality**
>
> I prioritize quality in every aspect of my life.
>
> My relationships are meaningful and enriching.
>
> I choose excellence in my work and personal endeavors.
>
> I invest my time and energy in things that matter.
>
> My life is filled with high-quality experiences and connections.

The Practice of Quality

Quality is about making deliberate choices that enhance the richness and depth of your life. It's about valuing the things that bring genuine happiness and fulfillment and letting go of what doesn't serve your highest good. By focusing on quality, you create a life that is not only successful but also deeply satisfying and meaningful.

As you embrace the enriching world of Quality, remember that a life well-lived is one filled with intentional choices and meaningful experiences. By prioritizing quality in your relationships, work, and personal growth, you create a life that is beautiful, fulfilling, and deeply satisfying. Let quality be your guide, helping you craft a life of excellence and joy.

What is Resilience? Next, we'll discover how to build resilience and bounce back from life's challenges with strength and grace. Let's learn how to embrace resilience.

Chapter Eighteen: R – Resilience

Building Resilience and Overcoming Challenges

Welcome to the empowering world of **RESILIENCE!**

Imagine yourself as a mighty oak tree, standing tall and strong despite the storms that come your way. Resilience is about your ability to withstand and recover from adversity, challenges, and setbacks. It's the strength and flexibility that allow you to bounce back from difficult situations and continue moving forward with determination and hope.

What is Resilience?

Resilience is the capacity to navigate through life's difficulties and emerge stronger, wiser, and more capable. It involves adapting to stress and adversity, maintaining a positive outlook, and finding ways to overcome obstacles. Resilience is not about avoiding challenges but about facing them head-on with courage and resourcefulness. It's a dynamic process that involves emotional, mental, and sometimes physical fortitude.

Why Resilience is Important

Resilience is essential for personal growth, mental health, and overall well-being. It helps you cope with stress, reduces the impact of negative experiences, and enhances your ability to achieve your goals. Resilient individuals are better equipped to handle life's ups and downs, maintain a positive outlook, and find solutions to their problems. Building resilience empowers you to live a more fulfilling and balanced life.

How to Build Resilience

Develop a Positive Mindset

Cultivate optimism and focus on the positive aspects of your life. Practice gratitude and affirm your strengths and capabilities.

Strengthen Your Support Network

Surround yourself with supportive and positive people who encourage and uplift you. Building strong relationships provides a safety net during tough times.

Practice Self-Care

Take care of your physical, emotional, and mental health. Regular exercise, healthy eating, sufficient sleep, and relaxation techniques help build resilience.

Set Realistic Goals

Break down your goals into manageable steps. Achieving small milestones boosts your confidence and reinforces your ability to succeed.

Learn from Challenges

View setbacks as opportunities for growth and learning. Reflect on what you can learn from difficult experiences and how they can make you stronger.

Reflective Journal Prompts

- Reflect on a challenging experience you overcame. What strengths and strategies helped you?
- How can you cultivate a more positive mindset in your daily life?
- Who are the supportive people in your life, and how can you strengthen those relationships?
- What self-care practices can you incorporate to enhance your resilience?
- How can you reframe a current challenge as an opportunity for growth?

> **Daily Affirmations for Resilience**
>
> I am strong and capable of overcoming any challenge.
>
> Every setback is an opportunity for growth and learning.
>
> I have the resilience to navigate through life's difficulties.
>
> I am surrounded by supportive and positive people.
>
> My resilience helps me achieve my goals and live a fulfilling life.

The Practice of Resilience

Resilience is not about being impervious to stress or adversity but about responding to challenges with flexibility and strength. It involves a combination of mindset, support, and self-care. By building resilience, you enhance your capacity to face life's challenges with grace and determination, emerging stronger and more empowered.

As you build your Resilience, remember that every challenge you face is an opportunity to grow stronger and more capable. By cultivating a positive mindset, nurturing supportive relationships, and prioritizing self-care, you create a solid foundation for resilience. Let resilience be your guide, helping you navigate life's challenges with strength, grace, and unwavering determination.

Ready to embrace self-care? How can self-care help you with self-love?

Chapter Nineteen: S – Self-Care

Nurture Your Well-Being Through Self-Care

Welcome to the nurturing world of **SELF-CARE**!

Imagine your well-being as a beautiful garden, flourishing with vibrant colors and life. Self-care is about tending to this garden with love and attention, ensuring that you are mentally, emotionally, and physically nourished. It's about taking intentional steps to prioritize your health and happiness, creating a foundation for a balanced and fulfilling life.

What is Self-Care

Self-care is not just spa days and manicures. It's the practice of taking intentional actions to care for your physical, emotional, and mental health. It involves activities and habits that nourish your well-being and help you maintain balance and resilience. Self-care is about recognizing your needs and making time to fulfill them, ensuring that you are recharged and capable of facing life's challenges.

What Does it Mean to Have a Self-Care Routine

Having a self-care routine means incorporating regular practices into your daily life that support your overall health and happiness. This routine can include a variety of activities such as getting enough sleep, eating nutritious foods, engaging in physical exercise, practicing mindfulness, setting

boundaries, and making time for hobbies and relaxation. A self-care routine is a personalized plan that ensures you consistently take care of yourself, promoting long-term well-being and preventing burnout.

Why Self-Care is Important

Self-care is essential for maintaining your overall well-being. It helps reduce stress, prevent burnout, and improve your mental and physical health. When you take time to care for yourself, you replenish your energy, boost your mood, and enhance your ability to care for others. Self-care is not a luxury; it's a necessity for living a healthy and balanced life.

How to Practice Self-Care

Prioritize Rest and Relaxation

Ensure you get enough sleep and take breaks throughout your day. Rest and relaxation are crucial for recharging your body and mind.

Engage in Physical Activity

Regular exercise helps improve your physical health, reduce stress, and boost your mood. Find activities you enjoy, whether it's walking, dancing, yoga, or playing a sport.

Nourish Your Body

Eat a balanced diet rich in nutrients that fuel your body and mind. Stay hydrated and listen to your body's needs.

Practice Mindfulness and Meditation

Spend time each day practicing mindfulness or meditation to center yourself and reduce stress. Focus on your breath, let go of distractions, and be present in the moment.

Set Healthy Boundaries

Learn to say no to activities and commitments that drain your energy. Protect your time and prioritize activities that nurture your well-being.

Engage in Activities You Love

Make time for hobbies and activities that bring you joy and fulfillment. Whether it's reading, painting, gardening, or exploring nature, prioritize what makes you happy.

Personal Story: Taking Time for Me!

I often speak about self-care because learning to love yourself is the foundation of healing and personal growth. When we take the time to care for ourselves, we naturally learn to love ourselves. On the days when I didn't have my children with me, I found myself feeling incredibly lonely. I had always been surrounded by someone – first living with my mom after high school, and then with my ex-husband. After 16 years of marriage, the emptiness and silence when the kids were gone felt isolating and depressing.

But it was during this time that I truly found myself. I had to learn to love the person I was without a partner. I did this by discovering

activities that made me happy and brought me inner peace. I started reading books again, like I did before I got pregnant with my first born. I also took solo trips to the beach by myself to remind myself of the beauty that surrounds us, and the beauty within us. When we learn to love ourselves and align with what we truly need at our core, our light begins to shine.

I've experienced the transformative power of self-care. There was a time when I put everyone else's needs before my own, which lead to burnout and exhaustion. It wasn't until I made self-care a priority that I began to thrive.

Reflective Journal Prompts

- What self-care activities make me feel most nurtured and happy?
- Reflect on a time when you neglected self-care. How did it affect your well-being?
- What boundaries do I need to set to prioritize my self-care?
- How can I incorporate more rest and relaxation into my daily routine?
- What small changes can I make to improve my physical health and energy levels?

Daily Affirmations for Self-Care

I deserve to take care of myself.

My well-being is a priority.

I nourish my mind, body, and soul.

I set healthy boundaries to protect my energy.

I am worthy of rest and relaxation.

The Practice of Self-Care

Self-care is a continuous practice of nurturing your well-being. It's about making intentional choices that prioritize your health and happiness. By incorporating self-care into your daily routine, you create a foundation for a balanced and fulfilling life. Remember, self-care is not selfish; it's essential for maintaining your ability to thrive and support others.

As you embrace the nurturing practice of Self-Care, remember that your well-being is the foundation of a balanced and fulfilling life. By prioritizing rest, nourishment, physical activity, and joyful activities, you create a life that supports your mental, emotional, and physical health. Let self-care be your guide, helping you cultivate a garden of well-being that flourishes with vibrant health and happiness.

Chapter Twenty: T – Trust

Building Trust in Yourself and Your Decisions

Welcome to the foundational world of **TRUST**!

Imagine trust as the solid ground beneath your feet, providing stability and security as you navigate through life. Trust is about having confidence in yourself and others, believing in your abilities, and fostering reliable and supportive relationships. It's the cornerstone of personal growth, healthy relationships, and a fulfilling life.

Why Trust is Important

Trust is essential for building strong, meaningful relationships and for cultivating self-confidence. It allows you to feel safe and supported, both within yourself and with others. Trust reduces anxiety and uncertainty, enabling you to take risks and pursue your goals with confidence. When trust is present, you can communicate openly, resolve conflicts effectively, and build deeper connections.

How to Build Trust in Yourself

Keep Promises to Yourself

Follow through on commitments you make to yourself. Whether it's sticking to a self-care routine or pursuing a personal goal, honoring your promises builds self-trust.

Acknowledge Your Strengths

Regularly recognize and celebrate your abilities and accomplishments. This practice reinforces your belief in your capabilities.

Be Honest with Yourself

Accept and acknowledge your true feelings, desires, and limitations. Self-honesty is crucial for building a genuine and trusting relationship with yourself.

Take Care of Yourself

Prioritize self-care and well-being. When you consistently care for your physical, emotional, and mental health, you reinforce the message that you are worthy of trust and respect.

Practice Self-Compassion

Be kind and understanding towards yourself, especially during setbacks. Self-compassion helps you build resilience and trust in your ability to overcome challenges.

How to Build Trust in Others

Communicate Openly

Share your thoughts and feelings honestly with others. Open communication fosters mutual understanding and trust.

Be Reliable

Follow through on your commitments and be dependable. Consistency in your actions builds trust with others.

Show Empathy and Understanding

Listen actively and empathetically to others. Understanding their perspectives and validating their feelings strengthens trust.

Respect Boundaries

Honor the personal boundaries of others. Respecting their limits and needs demonstrates that you value and trust them.

Be Honest and Transparent

Practice honesty in your interactions. Transparency in your intentions and actions cultivates a foundation of trust.

Personal Story: Learning to trust yourself!

This concept may seem simple, but we often tell ourselves we'll do something, only to talk ourselves out of it later. It might be planning to go to the gym, but then deciding you don't feel like it anymore. Or perhaps you start a diet, but by lunchtime, you convince yourself that you deserve a burger and fries because you had a stressful day. These are small but powerful examples of why it's hard to trust yourself. We are all guilty of talking ourselves out of something.

How can you believe in yourself when you don't keep your own word? Self-love means building trust in yourself, knowing that what you say to yourself is something that you can rely on.

Reflective Journal Prompts

- Reflect on a time when you trusted yourself and succeeded. What did you learn from that experience?
- How can you improve your self-trust? What commitments can you make to yourself?
- Who in your life do you trust deeply? What qualities make them trustworthy?
- How can you foster open communication and trust in your relationships?
- What steps can you take to rebuild trust if it has been broken?

> **Daily Affirmations for Trust**
>
> I trust myself and my abilities.
>
> I am worthy of trust and respect.
>
> I build strong, trusting relationships.
>
> I communicate openly and honestly.
>
> I trust the journey of my life.

The Practice of Trust

Trust is not built overnight; it requires consistent effort and genuine intention. By being honest, reliable, and compassionate with yourself and others, you lay the groundwork for trust to flourish. Trusting yourself empowers you to take bold steps towards your goals, while trusting others enriches your relationships and creates a supportive network.

In my own life, I've learned that trust is a journey that starts within. There were times when I doubted my abilities and hesitated to rely on others. But through self-reflection and consistent effort, I learned to trust myself and build trusting relationships. This journey has taught me that trust is the foundation of a fulfilling and resilient life, providing the stability and support needed to thrive.

As you build trust in yourself and others, remember that it is the foundation of a stable and fulfilling life. By keeping promises, being honest, and showing empathy, you create a trustworthy environment that nurtures growth and connection. Let trust be your guide, helping you navigate life's challenges with confidence and support.

What does it mean to be uniquely you? Next, we'll discover the beauty of embracing your individuality and celebrating what makes you unique.

Chapter Twenty-One: U - Uniqueness

Embrace Your Individuality and Celebrate Your Uniqueness

Welcome to the vibrant world of **UNIQUENESS**!

I want you to imagine yourself as a rare and precious gem, each facet reflecting your distinct qualities and experiences. We are each unique and none of us were born identical in every single way. Embracing your uniqueness is about recognizing and celebrating what makes you different from everyone else. It's about valuing your individuality and expressing your true self without fear or hesitation.

Why Embracing Uniqueness is Important

Embracing your uniqueness is essential for building self-confidence and living an authentic life. It allows you to honor your true self, pursue your passions, and make choices that align with your values and desires. When you celebrate your individuality, you inspire others to do the same, creating a world rich in diversity and creativity. Embracing your uniqueness also fosters resilience, as you learn to appreciate and stand by your distinct qualities even in the face of adversity.

How to Embrace Your Uniqueness

Recognize Your Strengths

Take time to identify and appreciate your unique talents, skills, and qualities. Reflect on what makes you special and how these strengths contribute to your life and the lives of others.

Express Yourself Creatively

Find ways to express your individuality through creative outlets such as art, music, writing, fashion, or any activity that allows you to showcase your personality.

Honor Your Passions

Pursue activities and interests that ignite your passion. Whether it's a hobby, a career, or a cause you care about, dedicating time to what you love reinforces your unique identity.

Be Authentic

Live your life authentically by staying true to your values, beliefs, and desires. Avoid conforming to others' expectations or societal norms that don't resonate with your true self.

Celebrate Differences

Appreciate and respect the uniqueness of others. Recognizing the value in diversity helps you embrace your individuality and fosters a sense of community and belonging.

Reflective Journal Prompts

- What makes me unique, and how do these qualities enrich my life?
- Reflect on a time when you embraced your individuality. How did it feel?
- What are my passions, and how can I dedicate more time to them?
- How can I express my uniqueness creatively?
- How do I respect and celebrate the uniqueness of others?

Daily Affirmations for Uniqueness

I am unique and valuable just as I am.

My individuality is my strength.

I celebrate my distinct qualities and talents.

I express myself authentically and creatively.

I honor my passions and pursue what I love.

The Practice of Embracing Uniqueness

Embracing your uniqueness is a continuous journey of self-discovery and self-acceptance. I know truly being your authentic self comes with challenges. It's about recognizing your inherent worth and celebrating the qualities that set you apart. By valuing your individuality, you build self-confidence and create a life that reflects your true self. Embracing uniqueness also involves encouraging others to do the same, fostering a diverse and inclusive community.

In my own life, I've discovered that embracing my uniqueness has been a powerful source of strength and joy. As a recovering people-pleaser, standing out as my authentic self was a concept I was not willing to conform to. It meant being different than the woman I grew up being.

When I felt the pressure to conform, I realized that by honoring my true self and pursuing my passions, I found a deeper sense of fulfillment. This journey has taught me that our differences are what make us beautiful and that celebrating our uniqueness enriches our lives and the lives of those around us.

As you embrace your Uniqueness, remember that your individuality is a gift to be celebrated. By recognizing your strengths, expressing yourself creatively, and honoring your passions, you create a life that is authentically yours. Let your uniqueness shine, inspiring others to do the same and contributing to a world that values and celebrates diversity.

When we talk about the need to be unique, it comes with dropping the walls we've built and allowing ourselves to be vulnerable. Our "V" is for vulnerable, which is a perfect segway to how vulnerability can lead to deeper connections and personal growth. Ready to embrace your vulnerability?

Chapter Twenty-Two:
V - Vulnerability

Embracing Vulnerability as a Strength

Welcome to the courageous world of **VULNERABILITY!**

Imagine vulnerability as the open sky, vast and boundless, allowing you to soar freely. Being vulnerable means showing up as your true self, with all your strengths and imperfections, and being open to connection and growth. It's about dropping the mask you constantly hide behind and revealing your authentic self to the world.

Why Vulnerability is Important

Vulnerability is essential for building deep, meaningful connections and for personal growth. When you allow yourself to be vulnerable, you open the door to genuine relationships and experiences. Vulnerability fosters trust, empathy, and intimacy, creating a foundation for strong, supportive connections. It also promotes self-acceptance and resilience, helping you navigate life's challenges with authenticity and courage.

The Connection Between Uniqueness and Vulnerability

When you embrace and show your uniqueness, you must be vulnerable. This means letting go of the fear of judgment and rejection and showing your true self to the world. It's about being honest about who you are, what you feel, and what you need. By dropping the mask, you constantly hide behind, you allow others to see and appreciate the real you, fostering deeper connections and a more authentic life.

How to Embrace Vulnerability

Acknowledge Your Feelings

Allow yourself to feel and express your emotions without judgment. Acknowledging your feelings is the first step towards embracing vulnerability.

Share Your Story

Open up about your experiences, struggles, and triumphs. Sharing your story helps you connect with others on a deeper level and fosters empathy and understanding.

Be Honest with Yourself and Others

Practice honesty in your thoughts, words, and actions. Being truthful about your feelings and experiences cultivates trust and authenticity.

Accept Imperfection

Embrace your flaws and imperfections as part of your unique self. Let go of the need for perfection and accept that vulnerability involves showing your true, imperfect-self.

Take Risks

Step out of your comfort zone and take emotional risks. Whether it's expressing your feelings, trying something new, or reaching out for help, taking risks helps you build resilience and courage.

Personal Story: It's ok to be me.

Being vulnerable is one of the hardest yet most rewarding aspects of self-love. I remember a time when I kept all my emotions bottled up, thinking that showing signs of weakness would make me less capable or strong. To be honest, there were so many instances when my marriage was crumbling to pieces. But I realized that true strength comes from allowing yourself to be seen, flaws and all. When I began to open up about my feelings and struggles, I not only felt a weight lifted off my shoulders, but I also connected more deeply with others. Vulnerability allowed me to embrace my authentic self, and in doing so, I discovered a newfound confidence. It's in these moments of raw honesty that real healing begins.

Reflective Journal Prompts

- What does vulnerability mean to me, and why is it important?
- Reflect on a time when you were vulnerable. How did it impact your relationships and personal growth?
- What fears or concerns hold me back from being vulnerable, and how can I address them?
- How can I practice honesty and openness in my daily interactions?
- What steps can I take to embrace my imperfections and show my true self?

Daily Affirmations for Vulnerability

I am courageous in showing my true self.

My vulnerability is a strength, not a weakness.

I embrace my imperfections and show up authentically.

Being vulnerable deepens my connections with others.

I am worthy of love and acceptance, just as I am.

Embracing vulnerability is a continuous journey of self-discovery and growth. It involves taking off the mask and allowing yourself to be seen, heard, and understood. By practicing vulnerability, you build deeper, more meaningful connections and cultivate a life of authenticity and courage. Vulnerability is not a weakness; it's a powerful tool for personal growth and genuine connection.

In my own life, I've learned that vulnerability is a gateway to deeper connections and personal growth. Still today, there are times when I feel the need to hide my true self, fearing judgment and rejection. But when I begin to embrace vulnerability, I find that it strengthens my relationships and allows me to live more authentically. My healing journey has taught me that showing my true self, with all my imperfections, is a courageous act that leads to profound growth and connection.

As you embrace the power of Vulnerability, remember that showing your true self is a courageous and empowering act. By dropping the mask and allowing yourself to be seen, you create space for genuine connections and personal growth. Let vulnerability be your guide, helping you navigate life's challenges with authenticity and courage.

I love how the alphabet is truly guiding us effortlessly through the journey of self-expression and self-love. When we find our Uniqueness and can drop the mask allowing us to be vulnerable, we can aspire to accept our Worthiness. Let's talk about what it means to truly feel Worthy.

Chapter Twenty-Three:
W – Worthiness

Embrace Your Innate Value and Self-Worth

Welcome to the affirming world of **WORTHINESS**!

Imagine yourself as a precious gem, inherently valuable and deserving of love, respect, and happiness. Embracing worthiness means recognizing and honoring your intrinsic value, independent of external achievements or validations. It's about understanding that you are enough just as you are, and that you deserve all the good things life has to offer.

Why Worthiness is Important

Worthiness is the foundation of self-love and personal growth. When you embrace your worthiness, you build self-esteem, confidence, and resilience. Recognizing your inherent value helps you set healthy boundaries, pursue your goals with conviction, and cultivate fulfilling relationships. Embracing worthiness empowers you to live authentically and with a deep sense of inner peace and satisfaction.

How to Embrace Your Worthiness

Practice Self-Compassion

Treat yourself with kindness and understanding, especially during times of struggle or failure. Self-compassion reinforces the belief that you are worthy of love and care. Remember to treat yourself as you would a dear friend who has come to you in need of your advice. You would hold space for them to be heard, so allow that for yourself.

Affirm Your Value

Regularly remind yourself of your intrinsic worth. Use affirmations and positive self-talk to reinforce your sense of value and self-esteem.

Set Healthy Boundaries

Protect your well-being by setting healthy boundaries that honor your needs and values. Boundaries are a powerful way to assert your worth and ensure you are treated with respect.

Celebrate Your Accomplishments

Acknowledge and celebrate your achievements, no matter how small. Recognizing your successes reinforces your sense of worthiness and motivates you to keep striving. You are your biggest advocate, so be sure to celebrate even the smallest of wins.

Surround Yourself with Support

Build a supportive network of friends, family, and mentors who affirm your worth and encourage your growth. Positive relationships are essential for maintaining a strong sense of self-worth.

Reflective Journal Prompts

- What does worthiness mean to me, and why is it important?
- Reflect on a time when you felt truly worthy and valued. What contributed to that feeling?
- What self-compassion practices can I incorporate to reinforce my sense of worthiness?
- How can I set boundaries that honor my needs and values?
- Who in my life affirms my worth, and how can I strengthen those relationships?

Daily Affirmations for Worthiness

I am worthy of love, respect, and happiness.

My worth is inherent and unconditional.

I celebrate my achievements and honor my journey.

I set healthy boundaries that protect my well-being.

I am enough just as I am.

The Practice of Embracing Worthiness

Embracing worthiness is a continuous journey of self-affirmation and self-acceptance. It's about recognizing your inherent value and living in a way that honors your true self. By practicing worthiness, you build a strong foundation of self-love and confidence, allowing you to navigate life with authenticity and grace. Worthiness is not something you earn; it's something you embrace as your birthright.

In my own life, I've learned that embracing my worthiness has been transformative. There were many times when I doubted my value and sought validation from external sources. My self-doubt has kept me silent in meetings when I wanted to speak up. But through self-reflection and self-compassion, I discovered that my worth is intrinsic and unconditional. This realization has empowered me to set healthy boundaries, pursue my passions, write this book and live authentically. Embracing my worthiness has been a journey of profound self-discovery and growth.

As you embrace the affirming world of Worthiness, remember that your value is inherent and unconditional. By practicing self-compassion, setting healthy boundaries, and celebrating your achievements, you cultivate a deep sense of self-worth that empowers you to live authentically and joyfully. Let the truth be told that I also considered Wholeness as my topic for "W". Embracing wholeness is a continuous journey of self-discovery and integration. It's about recognizing and honoring all parts of yourself and living in alignment with your true nature. When we feel worthy, we allow ourselves to feel "whole" as well.

I've discovered that embracing my worthiness is a powerful source of strength and peace as well. There were times when I struggled to accept certain aspects of myself, fearing they made me less worthy or capable. But through self-reflection and compassion, I learned to honor my complete self and integrate all my experiences. We all must embrace our flaws with just as much love as we embrace our wins. This journey has taught me that my worthiness is not about perfection but about embracing my true self with love and acceptance.

Now that we've explored the holistic world of Worthiness, let's move on to the next inspiring chapter: X-Factor. X-Factor is the unique qualities that set you apart and how to harness your X-Factor to shine brightly.

Chapter Twenty-Four:
X – X-Factor

Embrace and Harness Your Unique Qualities

Welcome to the dynamic world of **X-FACTOR**!

Imagine your X-Factor as the unique spark that sets you apart, the special qualities that make you shine brightly in your own unique way. Embracing your X-Factor means recognizing and celebrating your distinctive traits and talents. It's about harnessing these qualities to create a life of purpose, passion, and fulfillment.

Why Embracing Your X-Factor is Important

Embracing your X-Factor is essential for personal growth and self-confidence. It helps you stand out in a crowded world and pursue your goals with authenticity and enthusiasm. When you recognize and harness your unique qualities, you unlock your full potential and inspire others to do the same. Your X-Factor is your superpower, guiding you to live a life that is true to yourself and impactful to others.

How to Identify and Harness Your X-Factor

Reflect on Your Strengths

Take time to identify your natural talents, skills, and qualities that make you unique. Reflect on moments when you felt most confident and accomplished.

Seek Feedback from Others

Ask trusted friends, family, or colleagues what they see as your unique strengths and qualities. Sometimes others can see our X-Factor more clearly than we can.

Embrace Your Passions

Engage in activities that you are passionate about and that bring you joy. Your passions are often a key indicator of your unique qualities and strengths

Showcase Your Talents

Find ways to express and share your unique qualities with the world. Whether it's through your work, hobbies, or community involvement, let your X-Factor shine.

Stay Authentic

Stay true to yourself and your values. Your X-Factor is rooted in your authenticity, so embrace who you are without trying to conform to others' expectations.

Reflective Journal Prompts

- What are my unique strengths and qualities, and how do they make me stand out?
- Reflect on a time when you felt most confident and successful. What unique qualities contributed to that experience?
- How can I embrace and showcase my X-Factor in my daily life?
- What activities or passions bring out my unique strengths and talents?
- How can I inspire others by being true to myself and my unique qualities?

> **Daily Affirmations for X-Factor**
>
> I embrace and celebrate my unique qualities.
>
> My X-Factor sets me apart and makes me shine.
>
> I harness my strengths to create a fulfilling life.
>
> My authenticity is my superpower.
>
> I inspire others by being true to myself.

Embracing your X-Factor is a journey of self-discovery and empowerment. It's about recognizing what makes you unique and using those qualities to create a life of purpose and joy. By celebrating and harnessing your X-Factor, you unlock your potential and inspire others to do the same. Your X-Factor is your unique contribution to the world, so let it shine brightly.

I've found that embracing my X-Factor has been a powerful source of fulfillment and impact. I always thought my voice could never be used in meditation, yet I have recorded several successful guided meditations. There were times when I doubted my unique qualities, but through self-reflection and feedback from others, I learned to recognize and celebrate what sets me apart. This journey has taught me that our unique qualities are our greatest strengths and embracing them allows us to live authentically and inspire others.

As you embrace your X-Factor, remember that your unique qualities are your greatest strengths. Own them! By recognizing and celebrating what sets you apart, you create a life of purpose, passion, and fulfillment. Let your X-Factor be your guide, helping you shine brightly and inspire others to embrace their uniqueness.

Once you have embraced your unique qualities we call your X-Factor, it's time to honor yourself and focus on the importance of saying "Yes to YOU".

Are you ready to give yourself permission to be happy?

Chapter Twenty-Five: Y – Yes to You

Saying Yes to Opportunities and Self-growth

Welcome to the empowering world of Yes to **YOU**!

Imagine saying "yes" to yourself as the ultimate act of self-acceptance and self-love. Embracing "Yes to YOU" means prioritizing your well-being, honoring your needs, and celebrating your unique journey. It's about giving yourself permission to thrive and recognizing that you deserve happiness, success, and love.

Why Saying Yes to You is Important

Saying yes to yourself is essential for building self-worth and living an authentic life. When you prioritize your needs and well-being, you affirm your value and importance. This practice helps you set healthy boundaries, pursue your passions, and make choices that align with your true self. Embracing "Yes to YOU" empowers you to live a life that reflects your desires and values, fostering self-confidence and fulfillment.

How to Embrace Yes to YOU

Prioritize Self-Care

Make self-care a non-negotiable part of your routine. This includes physical, emotional, and mental care. When you prioritize self-care, you send a powerful message that your well-being matters.

Set Healthy Boundaries

Learn to say no to things that drain your energy and yes to activities that nourish you. Setting boundaries protects your time and energy, allowing you to focus on what truly matters.

Celebrate Your Achievements

Take time to acknowledge and celebrate your accomplishments, big and small. Recognizing your successes reinforces your self-worth and motivates you to keep moving forward.

Pursue Your Passions

Engage in activities that bring you joy and fulfillment. Whether it's a hobby, a career, or a cause you care about, make time for what you love and what excites you.

Practice Self-Compassion

Be kind to yourself, especially during challenging times. Self-compassion helps you navigate setbacks with grace and reinforces the belief that you are worthy of love and care.

Personal Story: *Saying YES to me!*

Saying "Yes" to myself was the turning point in my life. It meant making the difficult decision to end my marriage, not just for my own well-being, but for the future of my children. It meant choosing to prioritize their happiness and mine, even when it felt overwhelming. Saying "Yes" also meant going back to school to become certified, despite the uncertainty of what the future might hold. But in trusting myself, I also trusted that I would be divinely guided to where I was meant to be. Each step I took was a reaffirmation of my commitment to myself and my purpose. This journey wasn't easy, but it was necessary, and it led me to the life that I am living now – one filled with purpose, fulfillment, and alignment with who I truly am. This book is a reminder that when we say "yes" to ourselves, we step into the power of becoming the YOU we are meant to be.

Reflective Journal Prompts

- What does saying yes to myself look like, and why is it important?
- Reflect on a time when you prioritized your needs and well-being. How did it impact your life?
- What boundaries do I need to set to protect my energy and focus on what matters?
- How can I celebrate my achievements and honor my journey more often?
- What passions and activities bring me joy, and how can I incorporate them into my daily life?

> **Daily Affirmations for Yes to YOU**
>
> I say yes to my needs and well-being.
>
> I am worthy of love, success, and happiness.
>
> I celebrate my unique journey and accomplishments.
>
> I prioritize self-care and set healthy boundaries.
>
> I embrace my passions and live authentically.

The Practice of Saying Yes to YOU

Saying yes to yourself is a continuous journey of self-discovery and self-affirmation. It's about recognizing your worth and making choices that honor your true self. By embracing "Yes to YOU," you create a life that is aligned with your desires and values, fostering self-confidence and fulfillment. This practice empowers you to live authentically and inspires others to do the same.

In my own life, embracing "Yes to YOU" has been a transformative journey. There were times when I struggled to prioritize my needs and felt overwhelmed by the demands of others. But by learning to say yes to myself, I discovered a deeper sense of self-worth and happiness. This journey has taught me that prioritizing my well-being is not selfish but essential for living a fulfilling and balanced life.

As you embrace the empowering world of Yes to YOU, remember that prioritizing your well-being and saying yes to yourself is a powerful act of self-love. By honoring your needs, setting healthy boundaries, and celebrating your unique journey, you create a life that reflects your true self. Let "Yes to YOU" be your guide, helping you live authentically and inspiring others to do the same.

As we journey from Yes to YOU, where we embrace self-acceptance and prioritize our well-being, we naturally move towards a state of tranquility and inner peace. By saying yes to ourselves and honoring our needs, we create a foundation of self-love and confidence that allows us to live authentically and joyfully. This sense of alignment and fulfillment sets the stage for the next chapter: Zen. Embracing Zen helps us cultivate mindfulness and simplicity, bringing calm and balance into our lives. Let's now turn the page and explore how to nurture inner peace through the practice of Zen.

Chapter Twenty-Six: Z – Zen

Achieving a State of Inner Peace and Balance

Welcome to the tranquil world of **ZEN**!

Imagine your mind as a serene, still pond, reflecting the beauty and calmness around it. Zen is about cultivating inner peace, simplicity, and mindfulness in your daily life. It's about finding balance and harmony within yourself and embracing a state of calm amidst life's chaos.

Why Zen is Important?

Zen is essential for mental and emotional well-being. It helps reduce stress, improve focus, and promote a sense of tranquility and balance. By practicing Zen, you create a peaceful inner space that allows you to navigate life's challenges with grace and clarity. Zen encourages you to live in the present moment, fully experiencing and appreciating each moment as it comes.

How to Cultivate Zen

Practice Mindfulness

Engage in mindfulness practices that help you stay present and fully aware of your surroundings and experiences. This can include mindful breathing, meditation, or simply paying attention to your daily activities with a sense of curiosity and openness.

Simplify Your Life

Embrace simplicity by decluttering your physical and mental space. Focus on what truly matters and let go of unnecessary distractions and complications.

Create a Peaceful Environment

Surround yourself with elements that promote calm and relaxation. This can include creating a serene space at home with plants, calming colors, and minimalistic decor.

Engage in Meditative Practices

Incorporate meditation into your daily routine. Even a few minutes of sitting quietly and focusing on your breath can bring a sense of calm and clarity.

Embrace Acceptance

Practice accepting things as they are, without judgment or resistance. Acceptance allows you to find peace in the present moment and reduces stress and anxiety.

Reflective Journal Prompts

- What does Zen mean to me, and why is it important?
- Reflect on a recent moment when you felt completely at peace. What can you contribute to that feeling?
- How can I simplify my life to create more space for calm and mindfulness?
- What daily practices can I incorporate to cultivate inner peace and tranquility?
- How can I embrace acceptance and find peace in the present moment?

> **Daily Affirmations for Zen**
>
> I embrace the present moment with peace and clarity.
>
> My mind is calm, clear, and focused.
>
> I cultivate simplicity and balance in my life.
>
> I am at peace with myself and the world around me.
>
> I find joy and tranquility in mindful living.

The Practice of Zen

Cultivating Zen is a continuous journey of mindfulness and simplicity. It's about creating a harmonious inner space where peace and clarity can flourish. By practicing Zen, you learn to navigate life's challenges with a calm and focused mind, embracing each moment with grace and acceptance. Zen is not just a practice; it's a way of living that promotes balance, tranquility, and a deep sense of well-being.

As you embrace the tranquil world of Zen, remember that inner peace and mindfulness are always within your reach. By practicing mindfulness, simplifying your life, and creating a peaceful environment, you cultivate a state of calm and clarity that enhances your well-being. Let Zen be your guide, helping you live in the present moment with grace, acceptance, and tranquility.

Conclusion

As we conclude this journey through the ABCs of Self-Love, take a moment to reflect on the incredible path you've walked. Each chapter has been a steppingstone, guiding you to embrace and nurture various aspects of your true self. From Acceptance and Boundaries to Zen and everything in between, you've explored the depths of what it means to live a life filled with love, joy, and authenticity.

The journey of self-love is continuous, ever evolving, and deeply personal. It's about recognizing your worth, honoring your unique qualities, and creating a life that resonates with your true essence. By embracing the principles in this book, you've taken significant steps toward cultivating a fulfilling and balanced life.

Carry These Principles Forward

Practice Daily

Make self-love a daily practice. Integrate the affirmations, exercises, and reflections into your routine to reinforce these positive habits.

Be Patient with Yourself

Understand that growth takes time. Be patient and compassionate with yourself as you continue to evolve and embrace your journey.

Celebrate Your Progress

Acknowledge and celebrate your achievements, no matter how small. Each step forward is a victory worth cherishing.

Stay Open to Learning

Life will always present new challenges and opportunities for growth. Stay open to learning and adapting, using the principles of self-love as your foundation.

Inspire Others

Share your journey with others and inspire them to embark on their own path of self-discovery and self-love. Your story has the power to uplift and motivate those around you. It's ok to be vulnerable.

A Final Note of Encouragement

Remember, you are worthy of all the love, happiness, and success that life has to offer. By embracing your true self and nurturing your well-being, you create a ripple effect that touches every aspect of your life and the lives of those around you. Keep moving forward with courage, compassion, and confidence, knowing that you have all the tools and strength you need to live a life of fulfillment and joy.

Thank you for allowing me to be a part of your journey. As you continue to shine brightly, may you embrace each moment with an open heart and an unwavering belief in your limitless potential. Remember, the journey of self-love is not just about reaching a destination; it's about embracing every step along the way. Keep nurturing your beautiful self, and may your life be filled with endless love and joy.

With love and gratitude,
Amie

More Resources

Your personal journey of self-love and personal growth doesn't have to end here. If you're looking for additional support, inspiration, or resources, I'd love to connect with you. Here are some ways you can find me and stay engaged:

My website

Visit my website at amierich.com for more information about my services, upcoming events, the healing membership and additional resources to support your journey.

Social Media

Follow me on Instagram @amiearich for daily inspiration, tips, and updates.

Join our community of like-minded individuals committed to personal growth and self-love on Facebook at https://www.facebook.com/beyondnumbing.

Are you on Pinterest? Me too. Follow me @coachamie

Additional Books and Resources

I offer a range of eBooks and resources designed to support you on your journey of self-discovery and healing. All of these and others can be found at amierich.com

Here are some of my other offerings:

Limiting Beliefs eBook and Workbook

"Limiting Beliefs" is not just an eBook; it's an invitation to embark on a courageous expedition into the recesses of your own mind. As we journey together through these pages, may you find the courage to question, the strength to challenge, and the wisdom to dismantle the limiting beliefs that have held you captive for far too long.

Healthy Boundaries: How to Say No Without Feeling Guilty eBook and Workbook

This insightful and practical eBook (and complimentary workbook) invites readers on a transformative journey to understand, establish, and maintain healthy boundaries that foster genuine connections and personal well-being.

Emotional Intelligence eBook and Workbook

Until we can identify our emotional triggers correctly, they will continue to rule over our emotions. This eBook will guide readers on how to deal with the triggers once we are more aware of their existence. When we can start to understand what triggers us, we can set healthy boundaries with those in our lives.

Self-Acceptance: How Compassion Frees You, Heals You and Leads You to Radical Contentment eBook and Workbook

Embark on a transformative journey of self-discovery and radical contentment with this eBook. In a world that often emphasizes perfection and external validation, this eBook and accompanying workbook is a guide that offers a refreshing and empowering perspective on the profound impact of self-acceptance and compassion.

Self-Love eBook and Workbook

Finding out who you really are and generating self-love for yourself is the most rewarding experience that you can have. That is when you live your life knowing who you are here to be. This eBook will show you practical steps with regards to developing self-love. It also explains what self-love is, and how it has been the foundation of all spiritual teachings.

Guided Meditations

If guided meditations are your thing, I've got you covered. Discover the various topics from Chakras, Forgiveness, Grounding and Connecting with your Inner Child. Check them out on the website, amierich.com.

I hope you've found the inspiration and encouragement to prioritize yourself in ways you never thought possible. Remember, self-care isn't a one-time act—it's a continuous commitment to loving and honoring yourself. By saying "Yes" to you, embracing vulnerability, and trusting in your inner strength, you unlock the power to become the person you were always meant to be. This journey is yours, and every step you take is a step closer to a life filled with purpose, peace, and profound joy.

May this book serve as a guide and a reminder that you are worthy of the love, care, and attention you so freely give to others. Now, it's time to give that same gift to yourself.

I believe in the power of community and continuous growth. Join our FB community to stay connected, share your experiences, and receive ongoing support and inspiration. Together, we can create a world where everyone embraces their true selves and lives with love and authenticity.

Thank you for being a part of this journey. I look forward to continuing to support you in your growth and self-love journey. Remember, you are worthy of all the love, happiness, and success that life has to offer.

Amie A Rich

SPIRITUAL HYPNOTHERAPIST

www.ingramcontent.com/pod-product-compliance
Lightning Source LLC
Chambersburg PA
CBHW061655120626
46550CB00003B/950